Other Works by Denis Roche

With Éditions du Seuil

Forestière amazonide (Amazonian Ranger), Ecrire 11
Récits complets (Complete Stories), *poems*,
Collection Tel Quel
Les idées centésimales de Miss Elanize (The
100 Ideas of Miss Elanize), *poems*,
Collection Tel Quel

with other publishers

Carnac ou les mésaventures de la narration
(Carnac or the Misadventures of Narration),
Éditions Tchou
La liberté ou la mort, citations de 1789
(Liberty or Death, Quotes of 1789),
Éditions Tchou
Anthologie de la poésie française du XVIIe siècle
(Anthology of 17th C. French Poetry),
Éditions Tchou
Eloge de la véhémence, sérigraphies de Bernard Dufour
(Homage to Vehemence, Silkscreens by Bernard Dufour),
Société encyclopédique française

Translations

Cantos pisans (Pisan Cantos), Ezra Pound,
Éditions de L'Herne
A.B.C. de la lecture (ABC of Reading), Ezra Pound,
Éditions d L'Herne
Conversions, Harry Mathews,
Éditions Gallimard
Trois pourrissements poétiques (Three Poetic Putrefactions),
Le Mécrit

ÉROS ÉNERGUMÈNE

EROS RAVING

followed by
Poem of 29 April 1962

by

Denis Roche

Translated

by

FRANK CEBULSKI

authorHOUSE®

AuthorHouse™
1663 Liberty Drive
Bloomington, IN 47403
www.authorhouse.com
Phone: 1 (800) 839-8640

© 2017 Frank Cebulski. All rights reserved.
©1968 Éditions du Seuil
©1978-1979, 2004-2017, Frank Cebulski

No part of this book may be reproduced, stored in a retrieval system, or transmitted by any means without the written permission of the author.

Published by AuthorHouse 11/09/2017

ISBN: 978-1-5246-8467-9 (sc)
ISBN: 978-1-5246-8466-2 (hc)
ISBN: 978-1-5246-8468-6 (e)

Library of Congress Control Number: 2017904287

Print information available on the last page.

Any people depicted in stock imagery provided by Thinkstock are models, and such images are being used for illustrative purposes only.
Certain stock imagery © Thinkstock.

This book is printed on acid-free paper.

Because of the dynamic nature of the Internet, any web addresses or links contained in this book may have changed since publication and may no longer be valid. The views expressed in this work are solely those of the author and do not necessarily reflect the views of the publisher, and the publisher hereby disclaims any responsibility for them.

Contents

Eros Raving 5

Theater of the Schemes of Eros 39

Reader, you tremble with astonishment! 71

Respective positions of the two lovers in February 1964 97

Misconceived Memories 119

Eros, Lymne Cycle 135

The Library of Congress 167

Iambics of Disaffection 201

Elementary Eros always a Little Near October 209

Eros Raving continued 221

"DEBRIS Fragments, Horrible Accidents" Nietzsche 233

7 Sensible Poems, without Conclusion 241

Poem of 29 April 1962 261

Biography and Bibliography of Denis Roche 281

Notes on Poems and Translation 289

Translator's Afterword: Love on the Rocks 317

Acknowledgements

Special thanks to Denis Roche and Éditions du Seuil for granting me the English rights for publication of my translation of *Éros énergumène*.

Special thanks also to Dr. Kenneth McKellar, Professor of French, King's College, The University of Western Ontario, for his friendship throughout these many years and his invaluable help with these translations. Any and all errors, however, are my own.

Cover image: *All Things Seek Their Own Level of Complexity*, watercolor by Frank Cebulski©2017. All rights reserved.

To her.
I would have dared to dedicate it to him,
if he had been found worthy of it.

Year VI.

A elle.
J'aurais osé le lui dédier,
s'il s'en fût trouvé digne.

an VI.

Lessons on the Poetic Vacancy

(*fragments*)

On an Idea of Alteration

Never having lost sight of the fact that he owes his progress to his enormous spirit to cultivate convention—to regulate it according to the incessant need that he has to support himself before everything—man, but only providing that he be alert *to this fact*, remains at the center of the emancipation of thought if, as said Novalis, *the state of criticism is the element of liberty.*

Chance perhaps willed that the necessity of convention rest first upon speech before becoming mixed with, *the onset of the game*, writing (but of what chronology are we certain?). A game, or a practice, or indeed the imperative of some *tracery* (whose modalities are forever unknown to us) brought about one day on some small Aegean island (for us as Western man, of course) the birth of a convention, *visible according to a given order by the dispositions of inscribed characters.*

This disposition of the written must have been at the beginning only a schematic means of establishing by a series of reflexive arcs passing the retinal (it is there, all *retinal discipline*) a thought progressing remarkably down the road of analysis or of "souls" or of tools. We know, however, that the most ancient mathematical texts were composed in verse, but we do not know what the most ancient texts of poetry spoke about. Fine. But what are we to deduce from this, if not, doubtlessly, that given the absence of known roots for the poetic thing, for us it cannot be a question of approving nor even of commenting on any enterprise of poetic theorization which would lose sight for an instant of the fact that I must be answerable above all to its own reflection, or, if you wish, to its autocriticism. It is, perhaps, a kind of justification by mistrust, but let us quite agree that poetry is not itself recognized as birth, that it is not recognized as work, that it is *no longer* known as science, and that it is never recognized as society. And concerning its relation to society—to its own society—it is the poets who bear the expense, if indeed they still persist in believing—in *wanting* to believe—that poetry and criticism are in opposition. These "artistes" of verse have for so long paid out, with no disrespect to their insurance or to their good reason, in the customary manner, that they could only see in our intention to *dis-figure the written convention* a truism or a provocation by a pauper. But how easy to call a truism that which one knows so well that one writes constantly as if one did not know it, and to neutralize, by calling it provocation, that which presents itself precisely as a plague falling upon the calculated provocation of today!

We say therefore that if we want to dis-figure convention, we must, above all, *speak against words. To drag them along with oneself in the shame where they lead us, in such a manner that they therein disfigure themselves* (Francis Ponge). That is the undertaking in *Eros Raving*.

Of Convention and Sur-Codification

To dis-figure written convention is, in writing, to testify in a continuous way that poetry is a convention (*genre*) at the interior of convention (*communication*). An establishment better founded of this state of fact could come to us from studies bearing today—it is one of the possible solutions, only one of course—on the first manifestations, at the end of the Middle Ages, of this intention to codify written conventions. Can not one in fact think that the *Leys d'Amors*, or the *Art de dictier* of Eustache Deschamps or also the *Art de Rhétorique* attributed to Molinet, only aim at neutralizing the effect of the possible overflowing of this convention by *freezing* it? All personal intervention thus banished (we will have to wait for Marot in order to resuscitate it to the great harm of the heirs of the Pléiade), one attends in some way a mass seizure, a flocking-together, of poetic convention. All masques (spectacle calling itself innocent) fallen away, everything that invites the reader rendered impossible, there remains only a naked code, coding and sur-coding the unity of principle, the unity of convention, the poem. When will this prejudice of the rhetoricians, at a point that it will be good for us to define one day, rejoin the essential effort to overturn everything, which the work of Lautréamont constitutes? What a dream it is then, this absolute divergence that would throw us beyond all of *them*, beyond *all of these*, these *relative contortions*, the flux-reflux of mundanities, the soliloquy-of-the-reflective-man, the metaphysic-of-the-song-of-dignity-conquered, and then the incantation, all shamanizings of objects without functions, all cruel avatars of this *poetic functioning* (FONCTIONNEMENT POÉTIQUE), for a long time now disqualified.

To note next, without doubt, that a confusion at the level of theory explains alone the overflowing of low lyricism as born of surrealism; the exploitation by the latter of the invented fantastic and of the reiterated dream (writing calling itself not controlled) serving as alibi for a kind of logorrhea of the *superior* imagination (nostalgia of the kind of immediate transcendence that one attributes with so much eagerness to poetic creation).

Tableau of the Avatars

The strict definition of the rules of poetic writing would only have meaning under this condition: to put at divergence the said avatars, or perhaps, over and above this (why not, which would explain certain of my procedures that some have called *collage* (?)), their critical utilization, in so far as they are elements borrowed from discourse.

A tableau of these avatars remains to be drawn up. Let us establish, then, some impervious graphs and let us count, let us recapitulate and let us order the entry in diagram of such madcap combinations in which we were so elegantly dressed (one day we must also tell to what point we seek out this clothing, and to what point we seek out that we seek it!) We must settle for that and be satisfied with it.

The fixing of such material stuff for critical investigation would have two consequences:

—poetry would be rid of the moral, affective, sentimental and philosophical exponents that overpower it today, poems being generally related to a *Good*, a *Use*, or a *Beauty*. To say and to repeat that we still speak now of poetry as we spoke about it at Madame Des Roche's or at Julie d'Angennes' for whom formerly the most celebrated *garlands* were tressed. To say and repeat always all the nostalgias so as to avoid that the verdicts of the people in high places remain very imprecise and very badly founded, these puppets of coquetry and of beautiful sentiment, never hazarding to demonstrate anything whatsoever, analysis being replaced by paraphrase and some jumps of beautiful language (they would even, it appears, put some of their pride in this).

—the possibility of explicating, of indicating some certitudes. In not knowing what it is that is sought, how is it that one can note with so much conviction the *success* of such and such a page? How explicate it without the critical support of a descriptive terminology that would not content itself with describing the contents (it is this paraphrase of which we speak and which is gangrene in all of them) but would describe also the container, that is to say, an ensemble of laws not known, governing (and without it being possible to do it on demand at this moment) some type of facts with dominant *pulsionelle* (the unfolding of writing, the rhythm of the arrival of metaphoric sequences and ellipses, the rhythm of the unfolding of reading, rhythm of themes, of their appearance and their destruction, rhythm of the structures of discourse, of their arrival and their disappearance, rhythm of disposition, of showing, of enclosing, of their possible imbrication and of their succession as so many *imprintings* (in the biological sense), *always functions of a social act that is the act of writing, and of another social act which is that of reading.*

To develop the idea of the trench that is between metrical rhythm and these rhythms about which I have spoken above. To consider that metrical rhythm has very likely been, at a given moment in history, only an invention of support, purely practical and of limited interest (stock-types to define: the concourse of improvised poetry, compliments of love, verbal jousts, popular poetry, etc.).

The End of Looked-At Poetry

The gesture that is in all written invention. Let it appear evidently *there*, but especially let it never betray itself otherwise than under the form of tracery disappeared. May this absence be seen as such by the reader. Without doubt rendered impressionable by some artifices in the manner of Kandinsky (his work with dots, lines, surfaces) … Therein would reside an interesting idea of dynamic space and not in the idea of the "possible multiple" such as one wanted to see it in the *Coup de dés* (the scattering there is historically limited; the sole interest present the Mallarméen idea of writing turning itself against itself *in the reading*. But that the levels of reading be in number

6, 20, or 50, what matter?). Pulverization was able to lead to lettrisation. For a time we had even engulfed ourselves in this bowel: the possibilities of the semantic function of writing have been blithely bludgeoned there to the profit of a mad proliferation of objects immediately consumable. And that is all. *Some of these objects were beautiful.*

The calligram is one of the possible forms of destruction of poetic functioning. For proof, the absence of the rhythms of which I have spoken (only one may remain intact, metric rhythm, which would tend to prove that it has never been integrated with the poetic function) and the absence of interest concerning the text of most of the calligrams (it being understood that I call calligrams all texts that tend to become figured). This betrayal of the figured written is manifest. A calligram is justified (that is to say, significant) only in an ideogrammatic writing (a truth that I intend to illustrate by some treatise on this genre). Some failures, therefore, just before the series *Eros, Cycle of Lymne* series Eros, Cycle of Lymne (pp. 126-127 and 132-133).

The End of Spoken Poetry

One of the goals of this little book is to show that there can be a poetry that is made neither to be looked at nor to be declaimed. Any poetry that could only be defined by one of these characteristics is but a counterfeit of poetry: "le lettrisme" has been the counterfeit that one looks at, metric poetry is the counterfeit that one recites aloud. We could show that all modern poetry characteristically counter-evaluative does not enter—nor can it be forcibly placed in the mould of a prefabricated metric. If not, how explain the specialization of metric forms, the short verses traditionally reserved for light poems, the alexandrine for ample sentiments and for debates with the soul, the iambic of Archiloque and of Chénier for imprecation (against fathers-in-law and revolutions), the ode for the vague longing of the lover and so on? Gratuitous form, that which would not serve as a cane for a manner of thinking, this form—would it exist?

We can destroy a metric, we can make it destroy itself by its own system (pp. 204-207).

For a New Scansion

To retrieve the idea of scansion. The latter should no longer be the art of evaluating the measure of verses, in their quantities (Latin) or in their syllables (French), but the science by all the means of the modes of pulsional alternation (pulsion being able to designate *the unity of energy in the poetic*). Certain pages of *Eros* might be studied at this sole level of the *pulsional rush*: some whole sections *make sense* when others, in a parallel manner, empty themselves without the least shock, and everything can be made and read at the same time that a certain number of *imagined layers* unfold themselves and whose thread even we follow very excitedly. Many other things to say, in taking certain poems as "plats de résistance."

Eroticism, or Fighting It Out with Everything

Eroticism is a word déclassé. Who still knows precisely of its remarkable power of excitement, of dis-figuration? It is spectacle abused, raving accomplished (he whose senses are deranged, being animated by a strong emotion) the frantic return to the pursuit. It is the just return of things while they are in the process of making themselves. To write is already a bitter livery, the cloak of Nessus, I should say, to be poetic. Poetic writing is a spectacle wherein one would like to make all enter, wherein he would like to see everything at the same time he is looking at us, that is to say, to be looked at as one sees us. Eroticism transforms (would transform, but yet of that I am so certain) spectacle and annihilates it totally. It is consumed in proportion as it unfolds itself, because *erotic writing is a complete and effectuated reversal*. We cannot play the role there. But I will say that it is the most accomplished form of irony, or of skepticism. And it is perhaps the sole means for he who writes not to be, not ever to be able to be, the dupe of that which he *acts out*.

In that there is this frightening idea (but if one knows it, what economy!) of the inveterate search for a something lacking, for a reality that one feels *as lacking*. And this continual apprehension communicates itself to writing by exaggerated plusions difficult to keep so not to amplify them, deform them, litanize them. Respected, they are perhaps an element of great density that leads to a conclusion.

Eros Raving

followed by

Poem of 29 April 1962

I had hoped to satisfy a little my love for her by giving her my bouquet, it was completely useless. That is not possible but by literature or coitus. I write that not because I am ignorant of it, but because it is perhaps good to set up frequently written warnings.

Kafka

J'avais espéré satisfaire un peu mon amour pour elle en lui donant mon bouquet, c'était complètement inutile. Cela n'est possible que par la littèrature ou le coït. Je n'écris pas cela parce que je l'ignorais, mais parce qu'il est peut-être bon de mettre fréquemment les avertissements par écrit.

Kafka

Eros Raving

\ who leads me in this place who had fear has /
Revenge who knows not to bite with the arm-
Band of death passing the cheek in order to thee ensleep.
Prairies artificial (ar-ti-fi-shes-all) rupture
In a natural manner always more this
Shepherdess, what prudences ignorances it required.
One of the classique bits, by cause it is all
Completely devoted to this commune parched and lifts it
At last I descend to the city to walk by
Chance. *Coeur* corresponds if they elect in m.
In mean time, if you are marxist... and in
This woman who is young, with whom thou art enamored
I mean that she is very sick, if one must
Kill her, but she thinks, and there you are although at the
End of a minute (not even) she cries: to thee!
Continuity without vintage...

\qui m'amène en ce lieu qui eut peur a/
Revanche qui ne sait pas mordre avec le bras-
Sard de la mort passant la joue pour t'endormir.
Prairies artificielles (ar-ti-fi-ci-elles) rompent
De manière naturelle toujours advantage cette
Bergère, quelles prudence ignorance il fallait!
Un des morceaux classiques, par ce qu'il est tout
Entier dévoué a cette grande ambiguïté, allonge
La joie, alterne cette commune sèche et l'élève
Enfin je descends en ville pour me promener au
Hazard. *Coeur* correspond s'ils élisent en m.
En même temps, si vous êtes marxiste… et dans
Cette femme qui est jeune, dont tu t'éprends
Je veux dire qu'elle est très malade, s'il faut
La tuer, mais elle pense, et voilà bien qu'au
Bout d'une minute (pas même) elle crie: à toi!
La continuité sans vendange…

So vengeance (but it is always this follows)
The miserable shackle of all silent coitus.
The quiver -- the harness -- falls back, noise, re-
Mounts and falls again against his thigh, noise, on
These, that he cites, notably the threefolding
(One more time this makes him sick, but these
Shocks are not at all strapped to the rhythm which
I take to say it) still a shock, with
The smiling and boisterous burst proper to the arrival
At altitude. The declivities, more dry, are
Prey to undergrowth ... very dense with the
Stamp characteristic, there are also cush-
Ions of juniper and the abardal, as they
Say, tough and deadly. Me I thee have
Made after the image of horse country = peaks
Crowned with snow that one sees on the
Walls of The White House, or typic-Hall-
Of-the-Grand-Administration-Building, in the Middle West.

Sa vengeance (mais c'est toujours cette suite)
L'attache miséracle de tout coït silencieux,
Le carquois—le harnais—retombe, bruit, re-
Monte et retombe contre sa cuisse, bruit, sur
Celles, qu'il cite, notamment le trifolium
(Encore une fois ça lui fait mal, mais ces
Chocs ne sont pas du tout accordés au rythme que
Je prends pour le dire) encore un choc, avec
L'éclat souriant et bruyant proper a l'arrivée
En altitude. Les pentes, *plus sèches, sont en
proie aux broussailles…* très denses avec le
Timbre caracteristique, il y a aussi les cous-
Sinets de genévrier et l'*abardal*, comme ils
Dissent, *coriace et vénéneux*. Moi je t'ai
Faite a l'image du paysage à cheval == pics
Couronnés de neiges que l'on voit sur les
Murs de la Maison Blanche, ou bien type Hall-
De-Grand-Bâtiment-Administratif, au Middle West

"2° Cabin of Agnes, in the mountains of
Massat (utilized by Erce). It's about a ca-
Bin milky. The shepherd, shod with clogs and
Wearing beneath his sash a bag of
Salt, holds in his hand the wooden ladle where he
Collects the milk. Cabin of stone roof of
Corrugated iron." -- On his side he has the same
Pretension as she he may also descend into an
Other angel...that we re-find everywhere mentioned
He looks a little at his glass, but this ease
Outside of her returns to him within the soul
--he asks forgetfulness from passions of breasts!
Boutique of his father for portal to walk
Himself by separation from men, desires
--*Don't leave please, we mus'*
--*Not burning arises set in swelter*; he
Turns back her arms (like goat) so that
Her torso being forcibly bent, he may
Bite her there where he de-vines her shaggy.

"2º Cabane d'Agnès, sur les montagnes de
Massat (utilisé par Ercé). Il s'agit d'une ca-
Bane laitière. Le pâtre, chaussé de sabots et
Portant en dessous de la ceinture un poche de
Sel, tien à la main le *lérou* de bois où il
Recueille le lait. Cabane de pierre toit de
Tôle ondulée."— —A son coté il a la même
Prétention qu'elle il peut aussi descendre en un
Autre ange…qu'on retrouve partout mentionné
Il regarde un peu son verre, mais cette aissance
Hors d'elle à lui retourner en dedans l'âme
— —il demand aux passions des seins l'oubli!
Boutique de son père pour le portail à pied
Lui-même par éloignement des hommes, l'envie
— — *Ne partez pas s'il vous plait, il faut qu'*
— — *Ne brille pas saute et se met en nage;* il
Lui retourne les bras (comme chèvre) afin que
Son torse étant très fortement courbé, il puisse
La mordre là où il la devine si velue.

She at the gangway, squeezing forcefully his hand
"sells his grain in order to eat the staff of life, we
pretend... (I) shrouded mixed with flowers
Of this seawreck but in his visit to hell
Tell me, if quick entry aspirant in view

or

Lights with stormy rays, watching her going a-
Way down the lowered fan fluttering her vulva
And passing through me make him for an instant detour
His desire dirty after sea ruin.
she recites this story of shipwreck of
Enshrouding, it is transport beyond a solitude
Nearly constant, where she throws herself out of this
Boat and runs towards the cabin already wet
She has even enough milk for me to believe
Here I am I'm coming! But what certainty?

Elle à la coupée serrant si fort ses mains
"vend son grain pour manger des p. de t., on
prétend…(I) ensevelie mêlée aux fleurs
De ce naufrage mais dans sa visite à l'enfer
Dites-moi, si vite entrée aspirant à la vue

ou

Lumières des rayons orageux, la regardant s'
En aller l'éventail abaissé battant sa vulve
Battant sa bouche à la même seconde (saccades)
Et me parcourant lui font un instant détourner
Son desir malpropre d'après naufrage.
elle récite cette histoire de naufrage d'
Ensevelissement, c'est l'élan hors d'une solitude
Presque constante, où elle s'élance hors de ce
Bateau et court vers la cabane, déjà mouillée
Elle a même du lait pour me faire croire
me voicy je vient! Mais quelle certitude?

For their story, I see these forces
Elect little by little a reality where we must
Enter. This form from now on in the field
For which I reproach myself by pecking the monument
Makes him assault, or in what domains
Might I one night see her pass
In simple disarray in the corridor or
Even (as she was evoking it one evening) dressed
In two or three pretty little things, on the im-
Portance of these things sound and costing little
Of me, separated from me, pit for heart/
Pendent 6 months but at first one week
The largest part of what she had of narrow
Is a sorry pittance to break in the middle
Still may she always be taken under the
Trace of her perfume, still may it be she
Who tells me to put out or light up/

Depuis leur histoire, je vois ces forces
Élire peu a peu une réalité où nous devons
Entrer. Cette forme désormais dans le champ
Dont je me reproche de grignoter le monument
Fais-lui assaut, ou dans quels domains
Se pourrait-til qu'une nuit je la visse passer
En simple déshabillé dans le corridor ou
Même (comme elle l'évoquait un soir) vêtue
De deux ou trois petites choses, sur l'im-
Portance de ces choses saines et peu coûteuses
De moi, séparée de moi, gouffre pour coeur/
Pendant 6 mois mais d'abord une semaine
La plus grande partie de ce qu'elle a d'étroit
Est une mauvaise pitance à casser par le milieu
Encore qu'elle soit toujours prise sous le
Calque de son parfum, encore que ce soit elle
Qui me dise d'étiendre ou d'allumer/

Misunderstanding is not in the text of the letter
Alone and versatile letters in thy attachments
Attachments it seems we serve ourselves better
In gold. Thou, accumulated result
Far from floods, but it's the farce that we
Poorly see (the readers) that I see pre-
Precisely (precociously) the flowers tumul-
Tuously in the drift of our violence. Sensibility
Intellectual, it is the chronicle most moving
The *hilarious* and the *bearded* seeking authorizations
      alone the essential nature of the— —
Genius, poetic thought from the tube where
You come to tell me with certainty a happiness more

                                              unachieved

Le malentendu n'est pas dans le texte de la lettre
Seule et versatile lettres dans tes attaches
Attaches paraît-il que nous nous servons mieux
En or. Toi, accumulé résultat
Loin des crues, mais c'est la farce que l'on
Voit mal (les lecteurs) que je vois préc-
Précisément (précocement) les fleurs tumul-
Tueusement en dérive de notre violence. Sensibilité
Intellectuelle, c'est la chronique la plus émouvante
Le *hilare* et le *barbu* recherchant les autorisations
      seule la nature essentielle du——
Génie, la pensée poétique par le tube dou
Venez me dire avec certitude un bonheur plus

                                              inachevé

Holding in certain cases, the future forms
Requisite, show me in dreaming, for your-
Selves no more exists than you remember
In telling him neither his misfortune nor my
Success. With unwearying patience
For I must participate in the work erected
Of thy coil of thy drunkenness of thy bandage
    this time some precautions in order to vary
Our manner. Say that she is to him momentarry-
Ly necessary, that the spoon of the couple-
Lings loses itself off and on in the most sombre
Woods, that ill-disposed story of her
Bust had given me more ravishments than a
Porch with some cyclists near she
Closes her eyes to make it better and to have me.

Tenue dans certains cas, les futures formes
Requises, montre-moi en rêvant, à vous-
Mêmes n'existe plus que vous vous souteniez
En ne lui disant ni son infortune ni mon
Succès. Avec une patience à toute épreuve
Car il me faut participer à l'oeuvre élevée
De ta torsade de ton ivresse de ton pansement
    cette fois des précautions pour varier
Notre manière. Dites qu'elle lui est momentané-
Ment nécessaire, que la cuillère des apparie-
Ments se perd par instants dans de plus sombres
Bois, que l'histoire mal intentionnée de son
Buste m'avait donné plus de ravissements qu'un
Porche avec des cyclistes à proximité elle
Ferme les yeux pour mieux le faire et m'avoir

In the name of all the inhabitants, the offer most
Little that the partridge continues, a number
Odd, all sorts of evils of the figure
With thy sewn legs on the fiery ro-
Ads with preparatives: that thou reduce to this
Very hour of the night ventilators and rooms
Lighted by lustres ravishing and feminine
At this very hour of the night. I retire the oil
That will nourish our lamps, she so unusual
Already, I knowing it, cannot but more alarm
     straining for that to admit that the two or-
Ders of woman, that the two organs that
Link them like aliments, like weeklies.
Flagging on her also, from rather far, the
Field seems absolutely new, embellished by
Other astonishing essences than those of the
Cedar and of the spray of aspidistra.

Au nom de tous les habitants, l'offre plus
Petite que la perdrix continue, un nombre
Impair, toutes sortes de maux de la figure
De tes jambes cousues sur les fougueux che-
Mins des préparatifs: que tu redoutes à cette
Heure-ci de la nuit ventilateurs et salles
Éclairées de lustres ravissants et féminins
A cette heure-ci de la nuit. Je retire l'huile
Qui alimentera nos lamps, elle si inhabituelle
Déjà, je le savais, ne peut qu'alarmer davantage
     tendent pour cela admettre que les deux or-
Dres de la femme, que les deux organes qui
Les lient comme aliments, comme semainiers.
Faiblissant sur elle aussi, d'assez loin, le
Champ paraît absolument neuf, enjolivé par
D'aussi étonnantes essences que celles du
Cèdre et de la grebe d'aspidistra.

Singing, or with a refrain, a young girl
Who has her right arm clasped with violence, her
That a brutal fright pierces then her virtue through
And through, is not the least display
Then of her protection. Near to the wave and to the
Bone which plows the woods, lightly above
This level of earth that seems to preci-
Piter with omniscience remarkable beings
And buckled with our plenitude. The oleaginous
At the lady's with the soft flesh, this lady has
The most beautiful buttocks in the region of *Solfatares*
Then lengthened out, reddening with the narrowness of
Our tediums and the illusion that she awaits me
sits drooling in order to whisper, paying
Thus for the right to occupy the bench.

En chantant, ou au refrain, une jeune fille
Qui a le bras droit embrassé avec violence, se
Qu'un effroi brutal traverse alors sa vertu de
Part en part, n'est pas le moindre attirail
Alors de sa protection. Près de l'onde et de l'
Os qui laboure les bois, légèrement au-dessus
De ce niveau de terre d'où paraissent se préci-
Piter avec omniscience les êtres marquants
Et bouclés de notre plénitude. L'oléagineux
Chez la dame à la douce chair, cette dame a
Le plus beau fessier de la région des *solfatares*
Alors allongée, rougissant de l'étroitesse de
Nos longueurs et l'illusion qu'elle m'attend
s'assied en bavant pour chuchoter, payant
Ainsi le droit d'occuper la banquette.

and uniquely fewer rays then in parting to tell:
O grains   little cock of sleep,
Any inundation, everything evaporated behind the
Curtain that once more surrounded the forgetfulness
Worthy of our coitus. Maturity with summer
Girdle that slides or yes full blouses
Forms made only to tremble without wind without seams
"Under her black hair, much closer to her
How unrecognizable she is, this
Week (situation unchanged) eyes, a
Style rigid and impersonal to lay out
Double mouthfuls
Hands behind her back so that I hold
Better her breasts *dazzling carmine*, chaste and
I with my melancholy, frightened, I empty myself
She is going to come, or will come, to seek me!

et unique moins de rayons qu'en partant dire:
O blés   coquatrille du sommeil;
Aucune inundation, tout est enfui dans le
Rideau que derechef enveloppa l'oublieux
Mérite de notre coït. L'échéance à l'été
Ceinture qui coulisse ou bien blouses rondes
Formes ne font que trembler sans vent sans raie
"Sous ses cheveux noirs, plus proche d'elle
Qu'elle n'est reconnnaissable, pour cette
Semaine (situation inchangée) yeux, une
Façon raidie et impersonnelle de mettre les
Bouchées doubles
Mains derrière le dos pour que je prenne
Mieux ses seins *carmin ébloui*, chastes et
Moi de ma mélancolie, épouvanté, je me vide
Elle va venir, ou viendra, me chercher!

Same idea to give of you. Please in-
Stall yourself but under some very long *sleeping cars*.
"I am sadly quit of this fraud..."
She had been loved in her time with a love
All being like *abjection in general* nor
Yet the inverse mechanism of her vulva
Shovelful of earth of the environs of this
Beach, because they slip away one be-
Fore the other, exhausting by the same the slightest
Paul Italian. Worn out but preceded by or
With a representation very quickly naked, but
Some naked young woman, apparently about thir-
Ty, reinventing all those who existed
Already. There are by consequence some attributes
Directed without her being aware towards
The double desire I had of her but so little
Handy/

Pareille idée de vous donner. Priée de s'ins-
Taller mais sous de si longs *sleeping cars*.
"Je te peins quitte de ce détournement…"
Avait été aimée en son temps d'un amour
Tout être comme *abjection en général* ni
Pourtant le mécanisme inversé de sa vulve
La pelletée de terre des environs de cette
Plage, parce qu'elles s'éclipsent l'une de-
Vant l'autre, épuisant par là-même la moindre
Paule italienne. Rompue mais précédée de ou
D'une representation très vive de nu, mais
De jeune femme nue, apparemment de la tren-
Taine, réinventant tous ceux qui existaient
Déjà. Il y a par conséquent des attributs
Dirigés sans qu'elle en ait conscience vers
Le double désir que j'ai d'elle mais si peu
Commode/

I do not see where you recover the image
The mirror, soiled gizzard of gentians
That she would show me other thing
… never attract more than you can love
Purity of La Marquise, in chains or hand-
Cuffs each time he takes off her
Nightgown of fleshcolored follies, and
That he consent again to this faded torso, if
Then, entering at my turn, I beg her to
Have in my hand the ownership of these dark
Baths…
To this end equally fascinating and
The orifices (origins?), lately the skin
Hunting clothes, the historienne sheds
By her game so impressive with allusions.
She, I must spread talc on hers
In effect the blow to me attests to it at last

Je ne vois pas où vous retrouvez l'image
Le miroir, l'éclaboussant gésier des gentianes
Qu'elle me montrerait autre chose
…tirez jamais tant que vous ne l'aimez
Blancheur d'la marquise, en chaînes ou cor-
Dons chaque fois qu'il la dévêt de sa
Chemise de nuit sur les revues couleurs, et
Qu'il consent à nouveau à ce torse éteint, si
Donc, entrant à mon tour, je la priais d'
Avoir en ma main la propriété de ces obscures
Bains…
Jusqu'à ce terme pareillement fascinant et
Les orifices (origines ?), naguère la peau
Les vêtements de chasse, l'historienne mue
Par son jeu si impressionnant d'allusions.
Elle, il faut que j'appuie le talc sur ses
En effet le coup sur moi l'atteste enfin

To harvest! To harvest! Plot fixed on long
Skirts!   SummerWas more impor-
Tant and conferred shepherds of best quality
Imprints on each his traits, effectively
A very beautiful man but with a ferocity and at first
So hard that on his knees on the plaster of the 19th
She only began to vomit at the 7th assault?
And I live by virtue of very powerful cadavers
Man of the theatre and the countess, she, of Trocaderos
Swap ravishing when she loses herself in a movement
On the trestles or of blood or the chords which
Lift the décor to the level of our look
Or OK then piano of the giant, the touch-that-makes-
Foliage, gift without contest of the narratrix
Her hands later open onto the planes
This widow will always make the ignorant/bury herself
And entomb.

A la glanée! A la glanée! Plan fixe sur jupes
Longues!   Été plus impor-
Tant et donnait des pâtres de meilleure qualité
Empreinte sur chacun de ses traits, effectivement
Un très bel homme mais d'une férocité et d'abord
Si durs qu'à genoux sur les plâtrières du 19e
Elle n'eut de vomissements qu'au 7e assaut?
Et je vis de vertus de si pussisantes dépouilles
L'homme de théâtre et la comtesse, elle, de Troc
Ravissante quand elle s'égare dans un movement
Sur des tréteaux ou du sang ou les cordes qui
Remontent le décor à portée de notre regard.
Ou bien alors piano du géant, la touche-que-fait-
Frondaison, le don sans conteste de la narratrice
Ses mains plus tard débouchent sur les méplats
Cette veuve fera toujours l'ignorante/s'enfouit
Et en tomba.

Moreover this cost of the voyage—very well! Very
Well! Arises slowly in French village,
More than the housemaids *an unconscious description*,
The lit-te-erasure of tropism, or the neat
Story as we dream it, this bed will touch
The port but no blood, no happy crack
My intention to outline the supports of virtue
Of edifices for outlines free
The horizon for a word that bathes in the
Rapeseed makes me tell what I was going to silence too
Unjustly: "who makes these rumors come and from where
Of my own camp, from these borders of my long
First chapter, so timid drawing me into the.
Hands of maids? Who can translate this second
Recording then even as I come closer
I pretend to address words to her?

D'ailleurs ce coût du voyage—très bien! Très
Bien! S'élève lentement en village français,
Plus qu'les bonnes *un inconscient descriptif,*
La lit-té-rature de tropisme, ou la propre
Histoire comme on la rêve, cette couche touchera
Le port mais pas de sang, pas d'heureuse gerçure
Mon intention d'esquisser des supports de vertu
D'édifices pour les esquisses dégageant
L'horizon pour une parole qui se baigne dans le
Colza me fait dire ce que j'allais taire trop
Injustement: "qui fait venir et d'où ces rumeurs
De mon propre camp, de ces bornes de mon long
Premier chapitre, si timide me menant dans les
Mains des bonnes? Qui peut traduire ce second
Enregistrement alors même que je m'approche de
Je fais semblant de lui addresser des mots?

He gets over thinking about this bosom of the North
(Whose sketch came from N) All that is a lot
Of hooey one must teach us about things more
Learned == he looks at *l'étude pour chêne du Tasse I*
dated 1957 and for which he is obligated to DB of New
York (in the same citation, with the thought in view)
His two aches to know that she wants him here and
Now and to rediscover under his hands the drawing of the
Breasts (the wild and quickly agitated bosom)
Appears to him rather radically dissimilar and
From which he tries to tell them he feels the suspense
Of winning   he senses the last posture of the
Morning and his lack of aggression flows away; he no-
Thing sees but a shelf of nrf----

Il se remet à penser à cette gorge venue du Nord
(Dont le dessin est venu du N) Tout ça c'est un tas
D'idioties on devrait nous instruire de choses plus
Savantes == il regarde l'*étude pour le chêne du Tasse I*
datée 1957 et qu'il devait à l'obligeance de DB à New-
York. (dans la même citation, de la pensée au regard)
Ses deux douleurs de savoir qu'elle le desire mainte-
Nant et de retrouver sous ses mains le dessin des
Gorges (la poitrine affolée et aussitôt remuante)
Lui paraissent assez radicalement dissemblables et
Dès qu'il s'essaye à les prononcer il sent l'attente
Le gagner   il ressent la dernière posture du
Matin et son manqué d'agressivité s'écouler: il ne
Voit plus qu'une rangée de nrf————

At the outset some small percussive sounds rise up
In an interesting movement of going and coming
Put—sounds are often official reports—
-orge bruised no longer finds her justification no
More must he suffer while with his own hands
He hauls up and down the nylon the weight
As charming mass that plunges vertically into
The material, conscientious as is after all her
Desire. The percussion is the spectacle, and once
The theater is stripped away, he will rest his brow on her
Inclined towards a certain number of thoughts directed
Towards them alone (that is she and me) directed towards
Their coupled image that the silence decidedly ef-
Faces/

Au début des petits bruits de percussion s'élevaient
Dans un movement d'aller et de venue intéressant
Mis—les bruits sont souvent des constats—
-orge froissée ne trouve plus sa justification ne
Devrait plus lui suffire alors qu'à pleines mains
Il tire les hauts des bas de nylon la soupesant
Ainsi masse charmante qui plonge à la verticale dans
L'étoffe, consciencieuse comme est après tout son
Désir. La percussion c'est le spectacle et, une
Fois le theater enlevé, il va lui rester ce front
Incliné sur un certain nombre de pensées dirigées
Vers eux seuls (donc elle et moi), dirigées vers
Leur image accouplée que décidément le silence éf-
Face/

Theater of the Schemes of Eros

Thêâtre des agissements d'Éros

In the guise of a dedication

In 1612 Father Valladier dedicates to Marie de Medicis the collection of his *Sermons of the Advent:*
"... As for the two crystalline fountains of milk that the bridegroom [*Song of Songs*, Solomon] describes as being so beautiful, *quam pulchae sunt mammae tuae*, how beautiful are your breasts! Which he describes as being better than wine, which he compares sometimes to grapes rounded to perfection and full of pleasing liquor, sometimes to twin fawns, lustrous, generously proportioned and fresh; how many wonders and sweets The Creator has hidden there! Where the blood sweetens and honeys where all the veins near and far in the body discharge by secret consent and occult transpirations their most benevolent nourishing influence, with such providence from wise and vigorous nature that if the mother finds herself depleted in ordinary nourishment she undertakes to consume herself to her base substance and ingest herself to the last drop of her blood, before leaving empty these miraculous springs of primary nourishment. That is why so often we see the complexion and entire well-being of nurses drained away through these two channels for the new constitution of their infants, two storehouses of manna, two well-springs of ambrosia, two fountains of nectar, two stalks of sugar cane, two jugs of honey, two balm plants, two clocks of the internal timepiece of the mother, two bastions and ramparts of the heart, two cascades of infantine nature, changed.

As principal source of generation, the bridegroom discovers and admires what she keeps silent within herself, *absque eo quod intrinsecus latet* (Caput IV, *Song of Songs*), besides what she keeps hidden within, which is his usual refrain, after he has extolled other beauties. Saint Jerome and other doctors understand it thus; and it is apparent that what is most hidden from us, and most incomprehensible in this divine fabric is revealed by her secret and discovered by her silence. If he now calls her *hortus conclusus*, an enclosed garden, because she is chaste; now *fons signatus*, sealed fountain, because she is devoted and dedicated to her spouse; then *puteus aquarum viventium*, a wellspring of living water, since it is from her we draw life; then *venter tuus sicut acervus tritici valatus liliis*, a sheaf of wheat with a wall of lilies, because she is discreetly fecund and fecundly chaste. A storehouse of marvels in animal nature, to conceive, to retain, to form, organize, foment, engender and return to life this divine animal that must rule all created nature; part hidden from view, but so much allied with the two rivers of milk, that by that, as by the quadran, she manifests her affections, her dispositions, her accidents and symptoms, and the fruit that she bears, whether it is conceived, whether it is healthy or infirm, whether it is male or female..."

En guise de dédicace

En 1612 la Père Valladier dédicace à Marie de Médicis le recueil de ses *Sermons de l'Avent:*
"...Quant aux deux fontaines cristallines de lait que l'époux s'écrie être si belles, *quam pulchrae sunt mammae tuae*, que vos mamelles sont belles! Qu'il dit être meilleures que le vin, qu'il compare ores aux grains de raisin de la vigne arrondis en perfection et remplis de liqueur agreeable; ores aux faons jumeaux du chevreuil, polis, rebondis et refaits; combien de merveilles et de sucre y a caches Le Créateur! Où le sang s'adoucit et s'emmielle où tout autant qu'il y a de veines proches ou éloignées en tout le corps, déchargent par consentements secrets et transpirations occultes leurs plus bênignes influences alimentaires, avec telle providence, de la sage et vigoureuse nature, que si la mere se trouvait frustrée des aliments ordinaries elle se porterait à digérer jusqu'aux métaux, et à influer jusqu'à la dernière goutte de son sang, avant que de laisser vides ces sources miraculeuses du premier aliment. Tellement que souvent nous voyons les complexions et comme tout l'être des nourrices découler par ces deux canaux à la constitution comme nouvelle de leurs nourrissons, deux magasins de manne, deux sources d'ambroisie, deux fontaines de nectar, deux cannes de sucre, deux cruches de miel, deux plantes de baume, deux montres de l'horloge intérieure de la mere, deux bastions et ramparts du coeur, deux cataracts de la nature enfantine, altérée.

Pour le pratelin principal de la generation, l'époux le découvre et l'admire en se taisant, *absque eo quod intrinsecus latet*, sans ce qu'elle a de caché, qui est son refrain ordinaire, après qu'il a exprimé les autres beautés. Saint Jérôme et autres doctes l'entendent ainsi; et il y a apparence que ce qui nous est le plus cache et le plus incomprehensible en cette divine fabrique s'entend par son secret et se découvre par son silence. Si l'appelle-t-il tantôt *hortus conclusus*, un jardin bien clos, parce qu'elle est chaste; tantôt *fons signatus*, fontaine bien scellée, parce qu'elle est vouée et dédiée à son époux; tantôt *puteus aquarum viventium*, un puits d'eaux vives, puisque c'est de là que nous puisons la vie; tantôt *venter tuus sicut acervus tritici valatus liliis*, une grebe de froment avec une cloison de lys, à cause qu'il est pudiquement fécund et fécondement pudique. Magasin de merveilles en la nature animale, de concevoir, retenir, former, organizer, fomenter, engendrer et renvoyer à la vie ce divin animal qui doit maîtriser toute la nature créée; partie cache à la vue, mais tellement alliée avec les deux rivières de lait, que par-là, comme par le quadran, elle manifeste ses affections, ses dispositions, ses accidents et symptoms, et du fruit qu'elle porte, s'il est conçu, s'il est sain ou infirme, s'il est male ou femelle…"

Theatrical Act of Love: 1st Chance

Beyond the effervescence of the instrument, simi-
lar to this badly turned phrase of our suicide
Together, at the Épée-de-rose—green ensign, we
See a little verdure of Sologne throughout—,
…not daring to give the heroine to verses so that
Nothing dies from such a singular agronomic error.

A flowery skirt that creates a Love at each step,
Hides from our eyes her ravishing charms; and this
Thigh like a chubby Venus… Has thousand beauties,
Has a thousand vibrant charms, finery, you substitute only
Some obstacles!…And this pretty shoe, which
Covers the foot of Hebe, of Venus, as provocative as it
Is, is it worth her naked charms?…
Thou hast lied about it, o flower of my lips, the
Beans and the bubbles of madness, thy tush straight
Up makes towards me some circumlocutions (use-
Less today) in the form of a corkscrew.

Théâtral acte d'Amour: 1ʳᵉ chance

Hors du bouillonnement de l'instrument, sem-
blable à cette phrase mal tournée de notre suicide
Ensemble, à l'Épée-de-rose—enseigne verte, on
Voit un peu de verdure de Sologne au travers—,
… n'osant donner de l'héroine aux vers afin que
Nul ne meure d'une telle agronomique erreur:

Une jupe fleurie qui crée un Amour à chaque pas,
Dérobe à nos yeux de ravissants appas; et cette
Cuisse comme à Venus potelée… A mille beautés,
A mille appas vivants, atours, vous ne substituez que
Des empêchements!… Et ce soulier mignon, qui
Couvre un pied d'Hêbê, de Vénus, tout provocant qu'il
Est, vaut-il ses charmes nus?…
Tu en as menti, ô fleur de mes lèvres, les
Haricots et les bulles de folles, ton cul bien
Droit fait vers moi quelques périphrases (inuti-
Les aujourd'hui) en forme de tire-bouchons.

In front of the parenthesis:

   Love is an affection
That, through the eyes, enters the heart,
And in the form of fluxion
Churns through the gut as a fart.

at the same time—it is a double-exposure in
time—, Agrippa d'Aubigné writes the *Adventures of
baron de Foeneste*. That is:
   "There are hard things that the poet has not interpreted,
what the eye discovers is a great multitude of
soldiers of the Alps well ensconced in the sun to repair
all the scars of their doublets made after the fashion,
to defrost their double moustaches—there you see
boot lackeys, a young lady who has a girdle between
her navel and her tits."

Double fiction: the writer and his age. The proof is
that everyone has already written it. Return to simple
fiction.

En face de la parenthèse:

    L'Amour est une affection
Qui, par les yeux, dans le coeur entre,
Et, par forme de fluxion,
S'escoule par le bas du ventre.

en même temps—c'est une surimpression dans le temps—, Agrippa d'Aubigné écrit les *Aventures du baron de Foeneste*. C'est-à-dire:
    "Il y a force choses que le poëte n'a pas interprétées, ce que l'oeil descouvre c'est une grande multitude de soldats des Alpes bien empeschez au soleil à recoudre toutes les balafres de leurs pourpoints faits à la mode, à déglacer leurs doubles moustaches—là vous voyez des laquais botez, une demoiselle qui a la ceinture entre le nombril et les tétins."

Fiction double: l'écrivain et son époque. La prevue est que tout le monde l'a déjà écrit. Retours à la fiction simple.

Theatrical act of Love: 2nd chance

                                  that
With the edge of a cotton table cloth I wiped
The weapon still sharp with thy stench;

   (here the citation of Mathurin Régnier
The wheat most easy for painters was com-
pletely ravaged when we relieved ourselves,
What poetry at last buried in a hole of
Clay does not like slits that are made for
Corks?—"Would you do me the
Favor, Mademoiselle?—Yes, yes, yes—
Of giving those two there… —I know, I know…"
I have deftly performed here "ronds-de-jambe", some
Spheres, some Pulcinelles, needing even the dunking-
stool sign of Puritan path,
Poetry, from a dairy maid, or from the leap that an
Augustine would make from her, will never redress it
So much for the outfit I handed thee when it
Only depends on me to postpone the assault (*sic*)

Théâtral acte d'Amour: 2ᵉ chance

                      que
Des bords d'une nappe de cotton j'essuyai
L'arme encore coupante de ta puanteur:

    (ici la citation de Mathurin Régnier
Le blé plus facile des peintres était tout-
à-fait saccagé quand nous nous sommes relevés.
Quelle poésie enfin enfoncée dans un trou de
Glaise n'aime pas les jupes dont on fait les
Bouchons?— "Voudriez-vous me faire un
Plaisir, Mademoiselle?—Oui, oui, oui—
De donner ces deux-là… —Je sais, je sais…"
J'ai beau y mettre des ronds-de-jambe, des
Sphères, des Pulcinelles, au besoin la balan-
çoire même signe de puritaine sentine,
La poésie, d'une crémière, ou du bond qu'un
Augustin ferait sur icelle, n'en revêtira jamais
Pour autant l'habit que je te passe quand il ne
Tient qu'à moi de remettre l'assaut (*sic*).

Theatrical act of Love: immediately after the 2nd chance

When we come to write phrases like those
Of the preceding page I am with the twigs
My most advanced companion thinking to amass my
Doubt on the pretext of a grinder in a
In a former companion (if you can accept the idea
Of paper and ink of the Chinese empire
In a century still more ancient than when there had
Been grinders) I fill the instrument of this phenomenon
born of a great number of springs common to my
Imagination. Like the foot posed precarious-
ly on the rim of the bathtub the left hand
Folding back the washcloth towards the creases which are
Level with her stomach. Etc. Of course, otherwise
What importance, of verdure or of the fountain?
Nothing would take away more of what I have told you
In surrounding your legs. A final tip: continue
With the following heading.

Théâtral acte d'Amour: immédiatement après la 2ᵉ chance

Quand on vient d'écrire des phrases comme celles
De la page précédente je suis avec des brindilles
Ma compagne la plus avancée pensant amasser mon
Doute comme le prétexte d'un moulin dans une
Dans une campagne ancienne (si tu peux te faire à l'idée
Du papier et de l'encre de l'empire chinois
Dans un siècle encore plus ancien que ne l'aurait
Été le moulin) J'emplis l'appareil de ce phénomè
ne d'un grand nombre de ressorts communs à mon
Imagination. Comme le pied posé précautionneuse-
ment sur le rebord de la baignoire la main gauche
Rabattant le gant de toilette vers les plis qui sont
Au niveau de son estomach. Etc. Bien sûr, sinon
Quelle importance, de la verdure ou de la fontaine?
Rien n'emporterait plus ce que j'avais à te dire
En t'entourant les jambs. Conseil enfin: continuer
Par le titre suivant

Interludes in the chances: about vowels and erosion

"I confess on the 20th that I find myself in a state of
death." *Some divine servings of the charming poem,* like
Baggage that the innkeeper is about to dispose,
Occupy fully some reflection. The thunder
Hardly came. I reconsider the advance
Brutal this time of the earth, the one wild-
Land the one whose people are dead where remain
The apricot trees where death but not theirs falls
Rooted in the spot place of capture grave
And so forth the word being nothing
Fatigue could it not be but a kind of
Discipline? Who would blind me when I
Write? The young neighbors of thy beauty
Would laugh at our debate not seeing
That our hands create divine servings of the
Charming poem

Interlude dans les chances: des voyelles et de l'érosion

"J'avoue le 20 que je me trouve dans un état
mort." *Des mets divins du poème charmant*, comme
Le baggage dont s'apprête à disposer l'aubergiste,
Prennent en plein quelque reflet. Le tonnerre
Est à peine venu. Je reconsidère l'avancée
Brutale cette fois de la terre, celle en fri-
Che celle dont les gens sont morts où restent
Des abricotiers où la mort mais pas la leur tombe
Creusée dans les pois lieu des arrestations fos-
Et ainsi de suite la parole n'étant rien.
La fatigue pourrait-elle n'être qu'une sorte de
Discipline? Qui me rendrait aveugle quand j'
Écrit? Les jeunes voisines de ta beauté
Pourraient en rire de notre colloque ne voyant
Pas ce que nos mains font des mets divins du
Poème charmant

"The Dipping of Jouy" or "the triumph"

I can find nothing more certain than the association
Of this first page of stretched canvas of Jouy
With the aggressive idea of dipping which Littré
Says is *a basin full of a bitter liquor*
In which the tanner dips hides in order to
Make them swell. D'Estrevaillières who, no longer
Fornicating, was eradicated from his estate of Eu,
Dressed while turning her back on me in a manner that
I admire at the same time her thighs and the perspective of
The lime trees. The odor of yellow flowers, hers
And the small coins of old tissue manifestly
Imposed on me to maintain a strict attitude that the
Dictionary, falling, did not interrupt. What more
Could I make of all this other than an aerial step that
Leads me into an unencumbered region of the room
Where the tissue rips up the glottis bystander
In other flowers, going and coming, thickening

"le Passement de Jouy" ou "du triomphe"

Je ne peux trouver plus sûr que l'association
De cette page de garde tendue de toile de Jouy
Avec l'idée aggressive de passement dont Littré
Dit que c'est *une cuve pleine d'une liqueur acide*
Dans laquelle le tanneur passe les peaux pour les
Faire gonfler. D'Estrevaillières qui, n'en forni
Cant plus, s'était effacée dans son domaine d'Eu,
S'habille en me tournant le dos de sorte que
J'admire à la fois ses flancs et la perspective des
Tilleuls. L'odeur des fleurs jaunes, la sienne
Et les piécettes du tissue ancient manifestement
M'imposent de garder une attitude stricte que le
Dictionnaire, tombant, n'interrompt pas. Qu'en
Fis-je du tout autrement qu'un pas aérien qui
M'amène dans une region désencombrée de la pièce
Où le tissue se trouve arraché la glotte passant
Dans d'autres fleurs, allant et venant, épaissie

After a prolonged exposure to the sun,
Curtains

But my sweet speech, confounding, whose worst
Existence *the second stein confirmed to her that*
It is true, on my inclination for my ruin, my
Absolution. Modest sinner, lewd words,
Nasty appellation, only a music enchan
Tress sustains her close to me. Her trespass
Resolved, the melody imaging my slow sweep
Towards the nearness of her existence, the chance
Encounter of the mixture of this colored vision
(colors of hair, of pots on stage)
And my malady, all this links my step
Without audacity, hyperbole, my enjambment of
Balcony on green balcony, in straight line I
Sustain myself like the landscape towards a fresh
Funeral batch, towards her tomb anyhow
(Detumescence-smile)

Après une exposition prolongée au soleil,
Rideau

Mais ma parole douce, confondante, où pire
Existence *la seconde chope lui affirme que*
C'est vrai, sur le penchant de ma ruine, mon
Absolution. Pêcheur modeste, orduriers mots,
Ordurière appellation, seule une musique enchan
Teresse se soutien près de moi. Son trépas
Résolu, la mélodie imaginant ma lente montée
Vers les près de son existence, la rencontre
Fortuite du mélange de cette vision colorée
(couleurs des cheveux, des pots sur scène)
Et de ma maladie, tout cela rejoint mon pas
Sans audace, l'hyperbole, mon enjambement de
Balcon en balcon vert, en droite ligne je me
Prolonge comme le paysage vers un nouvelle
Fournée mortuaire, vers sa tombe de toute façon.
(Détumescence-sourire)

The mares that carry me have led me there where the spirit was forced from my soul.
                    Parmenides of Elea

Les cavales qui m'emportent m'ont mené là où me poussait l'élan de mon âme.
                    Parménide d'Elée

1

The vaulting supported by who constructed it in 1000
Like being a yachtsman of the best stock, like he who
Grows agricultural vegetables, among others
The mountain, the chief herder, the blocked intestine
Of women in rows. Compared to this introduction
The declaration of fantasy on the décolleté
Of saints of very great virtue this too much
He loves
More and more in the face of verses that end
By *chance*, "carried away by the course of
Things," following this jetty that no blunder
Perplexes except in the animation that I
Make of her. And still if he allows me but

More than a few rhymes with *one* to abridge there
This fashion to lend me his accents, his
Primrose gut load, to my style…

The vaulting supported by who constructed it in 1000

1.

La voûte soutenue par qui met dans le 1000
Comme étant yachtman du meilleur cru, comme qui
Fait croître végétaux d'espalier; entre autres
La montagne, le berger en chef, l'estomac clos
Des femmes en files. A côté de cette introduction
La déclaration de fantaisie sur les décolletés
Des saintes de très grande vertu ce trop que tant
Il aime
De plus en plus en face du vers qui se termine
Par *aventure*, "emportée par le cours des
Choses", suivant cette jetée que nulle bévue
N'est intrigue sinon dans l'animation que je me
Fais d'elle. Et encore qu'il me soit permis mais

Plus que quelques rimes à l'*une* d'abréger là
Cette façon de me prêter à ses accents, à sa
Primevère lourdeur de ventre, au style…

La voûte soutenue par qui met dans le 1000

2.

:that we do not actually have Shelley's liver nor
This vapor that rises from the vapor that shoots
Out of the pump, that shades this road, in the hut
Parades, in the dance around. What she who writes
"The blacksmith farrier who has fire on his neck," the
Music in vogue the bed the wave the blanket and the
Carriage with blackbirds. At once unleashed and pushing
Ahead, our move, which the tintypes render mo-
Bile with the hot moist air that filters in from
The exterior, that then by mixing the
Words that he sums up in a formal meaning and phrase
That the air could spice up by itself in this
Bright blond ephebe of the packed truck—ford and mac
Clallande on tour their front shoving like a
Green pasture the war, who nourishes whom?
She who has no plumpness but, under her mons,
Space.

"The mobile moves not in the space where it is, nor in that where it is not."

:that we do not actually have Shelley's liver nor

2.

:qu'on n'a pas tout à fait l' foie d'Shelley ni
Cette vapeur qui monte de la vapeur qui s'élance
D'la pompe, qu'abrite ce chemin, dans la hutte
Parade, dans la danse autour. Qu'elle qui écrit
"L'maréchal-ferrant qu'a du feu sur son cou", la
Musique vogue le lit le flot la couverture et la
Berline de merles. A la fois dégagée et ayant de
L'avance, notre mue, que d'aplats reviennent mo-
Biles de l'air moite et chaud qui s'infiltre de-
Puis l'extérieur, que c'est donc en mêlant les
Mots qu'il totalise en sens formule et phrase
Que l'air pourra se ravigorter de lui-même dans
Ce bel éphèbe blond du camion bondé—ford et mac
Clallande en tournée leur front poussant comme un
Vert pâturage la guerre, qui nourrit qui?
Celle qui n'a de replete que, sous son mont,
L'espace.

"Le mobile ne se meut ni dans l'espace où il se
trouve pas, ni dans celui où il ne se trouve pas."

:qu'on n'a pas tout àfait l' foie d'Shelley ni

3.

Tie that is gone, such that if she
Not love me, to be nourished by these moralists of
This hair that she has recently coiffed in a completely
Different manner, my Apollo that you touch the la-
St chord of the way of the world and of sentimenta-
Lism, in the palms of the bath, the foot of your
Souls, like sandy wrinkles deploying your god.
Leave him and see again for some time
"the rocky entablature of the mountain, like
a nest of swallows the tempest shakes (Bret
Harte, Little Diamond Library 2nd series)
… My wife just recalled that she
had a visit to make, he said with a deliberate air
sitting down" Saint Nicolas to Simpson Bar…
This incident awoke a strange thing
The doorways where I sleep that are two and fertile with
Other stables, blonde horns by which he is comforted,
Virgil affirms, with the spirits to leave this predicament

Tie that is gone, such that if she

3.

Lie qui s'en est allée, telle que si elle
Ne m'aime, d'être nourrie de ces moralists de
Ces cheveux qu'elle a coiffés récemment de tout
Autre manière, mes Apollon qui touchez la der-
Nière corde du cours de monde et du sentimenta-
Lisme dans les palmes du bain, le pied de vos
Ames, comme plies ensablées déployant ton dieu.
Lui quitte et regarde encore pour quelques heures
"l'entablement rocheux de la montagne, comme
un nid d'hirondelles que secoue la tempête (Bret
Harte, petite bibliothèque Diamant. 2ᵉ série)
… Ma femme vient de se rappeler qu'elle
avait une visite à faire, dit-il d'un air délibéré
en s'asseyant" Saint Nicolas à Simpson Bar…
Cet incident chose étrange avait réveillé
Les portes où je dors qui sont deux et fertiles d'
Autres écuries, cornes blondes par où il est aisé,
Assure Virgile, aux esprits de sortir d'embarras.

Lie qui s'en est allée, telle que si elle

4.

<u>society only works when I paint it as</u>
When in the vast in-folio of the artist she
Finally turns to the golden arms of my beautiful sex.
Its connection (its rapport) when to the point
I advance the frightening flame turns with the short st-
Raw, to the errant vomit that takes its turn at the bul-
wark, at the two-way mirror of events; at…
send the bill for pitiful causes, in the
Drops of rain and yelps, the lark
Bobbling its head forward towards those she
Perceives on the raft the raftmen those
Who still suffer perhaps the doubtful combat
Of others. These that the old romances predict?
The signal, cast by the small sea flags
Are enough to give me the illusion of turning towards
The condition of he who knows how to consider, who

<u>society only works when I paint it as</u>

4.

la société ne marche que quand j'la peins que
Quand dans le vaste in-folio de l'artiste elle
enfin tourne aux bras d'or de mon beau couchant.
Son rapprochement (son rapport) quand d'la p.te
J'avance l'affreuse flame tourne à la courte pa-
ille, au vomito errant qui fait son tour des pa-
vois, à la glace sans tain de l'événement; à…
envoie le bec pour les dommages causés, dans les
Gouttes de la pluie et les aboiements, l'alouette
Faisant marcher sa tête en avant vers ceux qu'elle
Aperçoit sur le radeau les hommes du radeau ceux
Qui subissent encore peut-être l'combat douteux
Des autres. Celles que les romans prêviennent?
Le signal, lancé par de petits drapeaux marins
Suffit à me rendre l'illusion à me tourner vers
La condition de celui qui sait considérer, qui

la société ne marche qu quand j'la peins que

5.

<u>"She took literally my verses!" The eye not</u>
It is not permitted me, that the eye be blessed!
You offer to God sometimes your anguish,
Only at the balcony, talking, your gaze fixed on
These panels, christian in high flight and we ascend
Together towards the prairie of the "guess how much I
Am happy?" Only the peacocks, of the ot-
Her side of the water I beg the forms of the plot
The flank, his, some seconds in the
In the flow in the flow of boredom, fragments of
f. that caress us the feet the blood of our
Edition broken like a loaf of deficiencies? Fail
Finally, the lust of the bed that we miss
Together as much as the housewife her garlic.

<u>"She took literally my verses!" The eye not</u>

5.

"Elle eût pris au mot mes vers!" L'oeil ne
Me le permet pas, que l'oeil soit béni!
Vous offriez à Dieu quelquefois vos angoisses,
Seule au balcon, disant, le regard fixé sur
Ces panneaux, chrétienne de haut vol et montons
Ensemble vers la prairie du "devine combien je
Suis heureuse?" Les paons seulement, d'l'au-
Tre côté de l'eau je supplie les formes du plan
Le flanc, le sien, quelques secondes dans les
Dans les flots dans les flots d'ennui, bris des
f. qui nous caressent les pieds le sang de notre
Edition rompu comme un pain de carence? Echue
A la fin, la foudre du lit qui nous manqué à
Tous deux: pas plus d'ail que de femme.

"Elle eût pris au mot mes vers!" L'oeil ne

Reader, you tremble with astonishment! …

Lectrice, tu frémis d'étonnement! …

In this affair notice
That she never undressed
Is this not true? You tell me OB.

End of *Ovide in Good Humor*
by d'Assoucy.

En cette affaire l'on remarque
Qu'elle n'avait rien dérobé
Est-il pas vray? Dîtes OB.

fin d'*Ovide en belle humeur*
de d'Assoucy.

First bad color: "general ease"

Rose said to me with amazement:— "I love these
Old rock songs" (and snuggling into
My arms), "where one does not give love a
Janseniste importance."   This is what she
Told me, thus I interpret it in broaching
This immense terrace, a resemblance to if not
Deceived, now without end nor spirit na-
Tural, always short of a frame and of
Thy wing, Theosophy... Once my
Torments flew back, and I could not
Stop thinking about the sorrowful accidents that
Happened to her, she shows in her
Night elegancies how many of them she has seen
Which dark surge secretly and long,
Following the method of the melancholy tablecloth
The odor of fields makes her more denuded
Without however my hiding that we part
Or that we sleep together, in friendship.

Première mauvaise couleur: "l'aise générale".

*Rose me dit avec étonnement: — "J'aime ces
Chansons de vieille roche"* (*et se penchant dans
Mes bras*), *"où l'on ne donne pas à l'amour une
Importance janséniste."*   Ce qu'elle
Me dit, ainsi je l'interprète en approchant de
Cette terrasse immense, une resemblance à s'y
Méprendre, maintenant sans fond ni esprit na-
Turel, toujours à court d'une bordure et de
Ton aile, Théosophie… Autrefois mes
Douleurs revolaient, et je ne pouvais
M'empêcher de penser aux tristes accidents qui
Lui êtaient arrivés, elle montre dans ses
Elêgances de nuit combien elle en a vues
Qui fonçaient secrètement et longuement,
Suivant la méthode de la nappe mélancolique
L'odeur des champs la fait plus déshabillée
Sans toutefois me cacher que nous partons
Ou que nous couchons ensemble, à l'amiable.

Second bad color: "clear ideas."

What an idea to want to tar that which only
Virtue conceals? History after Bec-d'Ambez?
"So that the stain remains forever" (Trad. 1817),
The only one that was promised enc------------
In solution in thy flow, fertile my
Soft prick teased out in her where Barrett
Goes too far because of the pressure of circumstances
Even calming down, all well seen, by the machinery
—where you are in it, that returns a little!
My mistress and we begin well with
Heaviness, with thy soul, with thy head,
Then nothing more than the relaxed life, pockmarked
This girl about whom we speak, by a single step
Quitting the horizon thy enormous mons, and
Another step heavily menacing the heiress
Because once again I simply see her
Cover an absurd appearance. Rip that apart, with
Our thanks.

Deuxième mauvaise couleur: "les idées claires."

quelle idée de vouloir goudronner ce que la
Vertu seule recèle? L'histoire au Bec-d'Ambez?
"Que la marque y restait toujours" (Trad. 1817),
La seule qui fût permise enc--------------------------
En solution dans ton flot, fertile mon
Mol élancement démêlé en elle où Barrett
Va trop loin par la pression des circonstances.
Même apaisement, tout bien vu, par la machinerie.
--où vous en êtes, cela revient un peu!
Ma maîtresse et nous commençons bien avec
Lourdeur, avec ton âme, avec ton citron,
Puis plus rien que la vie assouplie, grêle
Cette fille dont nous parlons, par un seul pas
Quittant l'horizon ton bas-ventre énorme, et
Un autre pas lourdement menaçant l'héritière
Parce qu'encore une fois simplement je la regarde
Revêtir une apparence saugrenue. Dêchire-la, à
Notre merci.

The third bad color: "the three of
The Swing."

"… See my nothingness, in the course of all
This anatomy of myself! … (says Rétif)
Concerning the disturbed again, if the nerves are not
Intact, etc. surpassing in beauty all
Shepherdesses attending sweetly the name of the servant
And the evening hinders me from taking freely and the
Cause and the essence of other roses that she
Without moving, only a clamor, so very
Soon, you would want more penis, but I
Stop myself, we see of what sub—tlety
Is thy conduct marshalling in me the attention to
This debauchery of three persons, beyond the bed.
Sometimes just as he was *stopping*, she then responded,
While the flame of his heart in the dome of the twi-
Light barely darkening his autumnal body
Doubtless for some time, one by one. Without
Doubt so strong of me, during all this time
Like what one must only revive a
Little, "the greatest pleasure that you
have ever had."

Troisième mauvaise couleur: "les trois de
L'escarpolette."

"... Vois mon néant, dans le cours de toute
Cette anatomie de moi-même !... (dit Rétif)
De l'émouvoir encore, si les nerfs n'en
Sont intacts, etc. surpassant en beauté toutes
Les bergères morfondues milliflues le nom du serviteur et
Du soir m'empêche de prendre librement et la
Cause et l'essence pour d'autres roses qu'elle.
Sans bouger, une seul clameur, tel tout à l'
Heure, vous le vouliez de gland, mais je m'
Arrête, on voit de quelle sub —— tilité
Est ta conduite en me détaillant les soins de
Cette débauche à trois personnes, hors lit.
Parfois jusqu'à *s'arrêtait*, puis elle repartait,
Alors que sa chevelure en coeur de dome crépus-
Cule à peine noircissant son corps autumnal
Sans doute quelques heures, une à une. Sans
Doute si fort de moi, pendant tout ce temps.
Comme quoi il faut seulement se relever un
Peu, "le plus grand contentment que vous
eûtes jamais".

"Tranquil temperament loving your terrible cry."

Tranquil temperament loving your terrible cry
Of pain, then each desirous of his accounts
"I do not make mention here of the fenestrated paper"
What can I say, each of my wor-

...the divine liberator wants to appear in his mar
ch, and we distance ourselves from him this manual under
Thy arm, this making on the right biceps, in
This book someone just gave me and for which I have
Complimented the translator. The word with tranquil
Temperament, the paper fenestrated (just after
The shapeless rolls (? with letters lar-)
And do I still know how to dare to write?) e,
Eh! in sign of the times

"Tempérament tranquille aimant votre terrible cri."

Tempérament tranquille aimant votre terrible cri
De douleur, lors chacun désireux de ses comptes
"je ne fais pas ici mention du papier fenestré"
Qu'est-ce que je peux dire, chacune de mes paro-

… le divin libérateur veut paraître dans sa mar
che, et de lui nous éloignons ce fascicule sous
Ton bras, ce faisant sur le biceps droit, dans
Ce livre qu'on vient de me donner et dont j'ai
Félicité le traducteur. La parole au temperament
Tranquille, le papier fenestré (juste après
Les rouleaux informes (?de caractères gra-)
Et saurais-je encore oser écrire?) e,
Eh! en signe des temps

It was the day when the arc of thorns had form.

It was the day when the arc of thorns had form
Formed the heroic bandage across thy mouth. Hard
Laying on bended knee, mouth abundant and like a
Horse the music descends the long containers
Of thy salinity. Enfantine thigh but sticky
In the widespread cavorting weariness nibbles
Our throat no longer a laughing matter, the one in the
Other the advantage returning always with the blood that
We spill—will spill—in like case, or such
Adventure in Carolina—freeway blowjob and towards
Tarots of sequoia— … It's that if there is not
A woman *who does not speak with impertinence like you*
There is not at the same time any men (I mean
Of those who are or say so in the way they
Employ it) who only defend that they are always
Well founded. This membrane of imper
Tinence befits me, I find myself very vigilant,
And the arc of the pencil follows

C'était le jour où l'arcade d'épines forme avait.

C'était le jour où l'arcade d'épines forme avait
Formé l'héroïque bandage sur ta bouche. Dure
Couche à genoux, la bouche à bas et comme un
Cheval la musique dévale les longues caisses
De ta salinité. Cuisse enfantine mais grasse
Dans le lointain les fatigues cavalant mordent
Notre gorge ça n'est plus d'rire, l'un dans l'
Autre l'avantage revenant toujours au sang que
Nous versons—verserions—dans tel cas, ou telle
Aventure en Caroline—autoroute pipe et vers
Tarots de sequoia— … c'est que s'il n'y a pas
Une femme *qui ne parle de l'impertinence comme vous*
Il n'y a en même temps pas d'hommes (j'entends
De ceux qui sont ou se disent dans l'usage de
L'employer) qui ne soutiennent qu'ils s'en sont
toujours bien trouvés. Cette membrane de l'imper-
Tinence m'échoit, je m'y trouve bien comme vigile,
Et l'arcade du pencil suit

"She drinks, she drinks! Admire the incomparable lady!"

She drinks, she drinks! Admire the incomparable lady!
Most hollow phrase—poetry which I no
Longer avoid—if now I may only hold you, my
Lady of the shallow air of the most hollow vestige———
In thy dirty alienation we could go col-
lect thy fresh apple   Come on, let's open your va-
gina to the air—and—You will be turned on, torch plead
Thou, here posing for eternity, thy photo on
Thy back, your breasts with thy skin of yesteryear. How
I did love you! She would drink fresh ass's milk!
Remove the garment above thy wedge as if thou hast
Hope of finding us somewhere else, fucking the air
Fresh under the few pines that complete this
Promontory, the house is empty but open and
We feel in spite of the cold from the sea the absence
Of the gardener and the solitude of thy ass

"Elle boit, elle boit! Admirez l'incomparable dame!"

Elle boit, elle boit! Admirez l'incomparable dame!
La phrase la plus creuse—la poésie dont je ne m'
Ecarte plus—s'il n'était que je vous serrerai, ma
Dame à l'air creux du plus creux vestige--------------
Dans ta sale alienation nous pourrions aller cueil-
lir ta fraîche pomme   Allons-y mettre ton vent-
re à l'air—et—Vous voicy allumée, brandon plains-
Toi, te voicy posant pour l'éternité, ta photo sur
Le dos, les mamelles de ta peau d'autrefois. Que
Je vous aimais! Elle boirait de l'ânon frais!
Ote le linge de dessus ta cale comme si tu avais
L'espoir de nous retrouver ailleurs, baisant l'air
Frais sous les quelques pin qui terminent ce
Promontoire, la maison est vide mais ouverte et
Nous sentons malgré le froid de la mer l'absence
Du jardinier et la solitude de ton âne

Nurture this conscience to a tender shoot

Nurture this conscience to a tender shoot
And to the bowels, to the wings raised in what you want
To take her with him him asking if this vow was
In accord with that of her family? The law of
It was an excellent point reached, between
Ribs 5 and 7, perhaps, under the whiteness?
For his size so grievously lustful so grievously seen
That he uprooted me "from the showers"
Springtime and autumn it's the same problem
As with the all white calf that escapes and goes
Everywhere, sowing his white terror that breaks
Nuns and woodwork. Then the wind being favorable
They spread out and remain there a great
Part of the summer, writing about bloody reasons

Elevée cette conscience jusqu'au tendron.

Elevée cette conscience jusqu'au tendron
Et à l'entraille, aux ailes dressées en veux-tu
L'emmener avec lui lui demanda si ce voeu était
En accord avec celui de sa famille? Le droit de.
C'était un excellent point atteint, entre les
Côtes 5 et 7, peut-être, sous le blanc?
A sa taille si funeste lascive si funeste regard
Qu'il m'arrache alors "des douches"
Le printemps et l'automne c'est le même problème
Qu'avec le veau tout blanc qui s'échappe et va
Partout, semant son effroi blanc qui craque
Nonnes et boiseries. Alors le vent étant favorable
Ils s'allongèrent et demeurèrent là une grande
Partie de l'été, écrivant de sanglantes raisons

".. int[ent] that he could not support his r[ule]."

.. int[ent] that he could not support his r[ule}
As much as our Heart, our hilarity, the magic
Song of the sibyl bundled in the sheaves
Rises with a comic grandiloquence so
Sweetly c...... I would laugh at the hailstone cloud if it
Were not this beautiful atmosphere where I feel
The amorous humidity and the incessant rain.
"But we have seen them, the women, coming together a
Few at first, with the sole interest of
Gathering together, or rather two if he did not see them."
Besides the earth together with the clods she digs
The loins assigning me the appetite of her soft step-
Over the leather of the seat of the car see
If the blond wheat feels at last the offense

".. int qu'il ne pouvait supporter son reg."

.. int qu'il ne pouvait supporter son reg.
Tant notre coeur, notre hilarité, le chant
Magique de la sibylle courbée dans les gerbes
Erige avec une grandiloquence comique un si
Doux c………. Je rirais du nuage à grêle s'il
N'était cette belle atmosphere où je me sens
L'humidité amoureuse et la pluie incessante.
"Mais nous les avons vues, elles, se réunir à
quelques-unes d'abord, dans le seul intérêt d'en
cueillir, ou bien deux s'il ne les voit pas."
Hormis la terre en sus des mottes elle creuse
Les reins me désignant à l'appétit de ses mol-
Enjambe le cuir du fauteuil de la voiture vois
Si les blés blonds ressentent enfin l'offense

"woman, the adorable treasure who thee"

"woman, the adorable treasure who thee
Designs, how happy I was to see you
On a protuberance as if the young girl would be'
Come this woman seated on a chair, and whom
I choke afterwards on her knees" Then, I
Straightening myself, stiff ugly stretched out, and
How many knew to find the skill to make you see.
The scaffolding beneath all this European primacy
"You love the scaffolding which supports her so fleshy
The wood that I exalt until she hilarious the
Velvet pinned on the bad side fulfilling
Such a fire
That he is no more the gravel to which I consent
That he would no longer know to believe other
Gesture of recognition than those mated
— "In her I have conceived" — He is ravished — "Die!"

"la femme, l'adorable trouvaille qui te".

"la femme, l'adorable trouvaille qui te
Désigne, que j'aie le contentement de ta vue
Sur une eminence comme si la jeune fille dev'nait
Cette femme assise sur une chaise, et que
J'étrangle à la suivre à genoux" Puis, me
Fixant moi-même, raidi enlaidi à m'allonger, et
Combien su trouver d'adresse à te faire voir.
L'escabeau sous toute cette primauté européenne
"Adorez l'escabeau qui la supporte si charnue
Le bois que j'élève jusqu'en elle tordant les
Velours épinglés sur le mauvais côté épanouissant
Une telle flambée
Qu'il n'est plus de gravier auquel je ne consente
Qu'il ne saurait plus croître d'autre
Geste de reconnaissance que ceux d'accouplés:
-- "En elle j'ai conçu" - Il est ravi. — "Meurs!"

"In the introduction of the precocious apple."

In the introduction of the precocious apple
Press thrown in quest of the fable
Firepricks of Bengal, and could one
Willingly then, go without being seen, swaddled
By the god of attire and of dandelions
     (the flowers, not the crocs!)
So to speak that, without them, he goes and he
Could well announce himself at your entry and
Cry to me after his victory still weighing on thy
Legs his victory of fish without fanfare!
Or very well then should I be less blind to the
Violence of knowing you are well mixed up with him?
Woman as you say in order that thi-
Ngs make themselves so simple it is necessary "that with jonquil tautness go"
"payment to see in her new dress, with her lips
Like round sheep that stray so that she be
Nice and full, or with her black stockings
That I cannot touch, that I will not be able to see
But in decaying. OK take them for a walk with him?"

"Dans l'introduction de la pomme précoce."

Dans l'introduction de la pomme précoce
Presse lancée à la recherché de la fable
Ments des feux de Bengale, et y pouvait-on
Zèle d'alors, aller sans être vu, emmitouflé
Par le dieu de l'atour et des dents-de-lion
      (les fleurs, pas les crocs!)
Pour ainsi dire que, sans eux, il va et il
Pourrait bien se nommer à ton entrée et
Me crier après sa victoire encore pesant sur tes
Jambes sa victoire de poisson sans timbre!
Ou bien serais-je alors moins aveugle à la
Violence de te savoir bien emmêlée avec lui?
Femme comme vous le dites pour que les cho-
Ses se fassent si simplement il faut "qu'à
jonquille étroitesse aille"
"dû voir dans sa nouvelle robe, de ses lèvres
De mouton rondes qui s'éloignent pour lui être
Agréable et remplie, ou bien de ses bas noirs
Que je ne puis tacher, que je ne pourrai voir
Qu'en pourrissant. Alors tu les lui promènes?"

"on a parcel that is reforested to the meadow"

On a parcel of land reforested in meadow
With stones raised in the clearings, landscapes, ruin…
He could not stop himself from sighing and acting
In the function as rescuer for six characters
The lemon tree as the model of his blond mount
"We understand this mountainous part, be
Tween several woods that constitute the annex"
In the pathetic purity of my limestone, high
<u>Vicdessos</u> at 3000 m territory in so large
A measure of thy popular yellow meat
We barely surpass the material of the brutal
Ruptures. Who prevents us from identifying here
Other thing than the celebration of thy consummation
Other story than the knocking of thy knees
In wonderful trial and error of the creative profes-
                                            sional
Caught up in the juice that you expose me to?

"sur une parcelle qui est reboisée au pré"

Sur une parcelle qui est reboisée en pré
Epierrement élève défrichements, paysages ruin…
Il ne put s'empêcher de soupirer et d'ouvrir
En qualité du secours pour six personnages
Le citronnier à l'exemple de son mont blond.
"On comprend cette partie montagneuse, en
Tre plusieurs bois qui constituent l'annexe"
Dans la dérisoire pureté de ma craie, haut
<u>Vicdessos</u> à 3 000 m territoire dans une si
Large mesure de tes viands jaunes courues
Ne dépassons guère le matériel des ruptures
Brutales. Qui empêche que nous nommions ici
Autre chose que la fête de ta consommation
D'autre récit que le claquement de tes genoux
En merveilleux tâtonnements de creation profes-
                                              sionnelle
La remontée dans le jus que tu m'exposes?

Respective positions of the two lovers
in February 1964

Enigmas

Positions respectives des deux amants
pour février 1964

Énigmes

An angel cut in two by a cannon ball,
and whose two parts are incontinently joined.

VOLTAIRE

Un ange coupe en deux par un coup de canon,
et dont les deux parties se rejoingnent incontinent.

VOLTAIRE

The eyes on tomorrow's raw story
And the prose employed one after the other impaled
Distressed with insulting me, at both of us
Measuring the dimensions of the crime.

He knew that his interior movement would
Only establish the dogma of a travesty
Could it be that by all this noise then
His fall would only become provocative?

Les yeux au lendemain nouvelle crue
Et la prose employée tour à tour empalée
Bouleversée de m'insulter, à nous deux
De mesurer les dimensions du crime.

Il sut que son mouvement intérieur n'
Erigeait que le dogme d'un travesti
Serait-ce que par tout ce bruit d'alors
Sa chute n'en soit devenue que provocante?

She has this candor insistence and their
Virginia tobacco as domestic prudence
As leaving to me repugnance and their
Parting could now be predicted (questions?)

Difficult parting, to whom would you want
The exhibition of examples fully dressed, it
Makes up a little for he who lacked depth
But the absence clearly saved him reprieves

Elle a cette candeur l'insistance et leur
Tabac de Virginie comme prudence domestique
Comme reserve à moi de répugnance et leur
Sortie serait devinée tantôt (questions?)

Sorties difficiles, à qui vous voudrez
L'exhibition des exemples trop vêtus, il
Fait un peu celui qui manqué d'êpaisseur
Mais l'absence lui sauve bien des accalmies

Ah! How you enflame my curious desire!

RACINE

Ah! Que vous enflammez mon désir curieux!

RACINE

The imminent moment when she stopped
Rush of the regions that carries us
To the place of the candelabra if yes the offense
This furious theft that deepens or haunts

Each exchange in the vileness of the
Haughty solitude would return to tell
How such a small or blue organ
Must move together in another body

Le moment imminent où elle est arrêtée
Surverse des environs qui nous porte
A la place du candélabre si oui le fagot
Ce vol furieux qui approfondit ou hante

Chaque échange dans la vilenie de l'
Hautaine solitude reviendrait à dire
Qu'a de tels petits ou bleus glands il
Faut emménager à deux dans d'autres corps

1844

"To write as one speaks is to destroy writing; to speak as one writes is to a-spire to the urbanity of the French language."

14th century:
"Who sleeps all night in his ear
And weeps in the bottom of a pot?
Who puts out the flame of fear
And combs the hair of a belch of rot?

Who hears the last jot
Of the crow at table?
Who puts the shadow of a sott
On the shoulder of a bottle?

1844:
　"Ecrire comme on parle, c'est détruire l'écriture; parler comme on écrit, c'est attenter à l'urbanité de la langue française."

14ᵉ siècle:
"Qui dort la nuit dans son oreille
Et pleure dans le fond d'un pot?
Qui éteint le feu des merveilles
Et peigne le cheveux du rôt?

Qui écoute le dernier mot
A la table de la corneille?
Qui emporte l'ombre d'un sot
Sur l'épaule d'une bouteille?

Among this assembly of individual
Felicities O long patience to display
Sound volumes of new characters
A surprise of all that we recognize

In order to dispose irregularly an
Escape at least provisionally they
Seek on narrow goats
The market of lies with shouts

Parmi ces assemblées d'individuelles
Félicités ô longues patiences à étaler
Volumes sains des nouveaux personnages
Une péripétie de tout ce que nous connaissons

Pour disposer irrégulièrement d'une
Fuite au moins provisoirement ils
Cherchent sur d'étroites chèvres
La halle à mensonge des coups de voix

Forbid first hand what respect transgresses
Impose carelessly what it lays bare
That her splendid backbone hold, recoil from
Him, lightly like an embarrassed person

For her it is there, suspended in our
Allocation of reality, shares of
Elegance, verses, pastiche of leaflets
Of ankylosis and the smile of the printer

Interdit de près que le respect franchi
Impose insoucieusement qu'il la vit nue
Que sa splendide échine va, détale sur
Lui, légèrement comme une personne embarrassée

Pour elle c'est là, suspendue dans notre
Répartition sur la réalité, parts d'
Elégance, vers, pastiches de feuillets
De l'ankylose et du sourire de l'imprimeur

Each returns to his chosen place without
any thing being in the least advanced.

Théophile Gautier

Chacun retourne en sa chacunière sans
que les choses en soient plus avancées.

Théophile Gautier

Young and abandoned to you
Release or awl but always
This game we give you
The harrow and the haven I leave you

Before the beet who acquiesces?
If I take fire in the waters of movement
A partridge without stitches, hot, clucks:
Lesson for who does not kill it.

Jeune et qui s'est abandonée à vous
Parution ou perce mais il y a tout le
Temps que ce jeu nous vous le donnions
La herse et l'abri je vous les laisse

Devant betterave qui acquiesce?
Si je prends feu dans l'eau du mouvement
Une perdrix sans couture, chaude, glousse:
Enseignement pour qui ne la tue.

Misconceived Memories

Mémoires méconnaissables

Everything that is so indispensable to
Poetry is precisely that with which it has
nothing to do.

Poe, *The Poetic Principle*

Tout ce qui est tellement indispensable à la
Poésie est précisément tout ce avec quoi elle n'a
rien du tout à faire.

Poe, *Le Principe poétique*

after lunch, two years after, although he haD
learned behind in front in saddle to un-
fold the tarp, to dream "is it he whom hE
would have wanted to be one day? No where
and during a happy moment after a similar lunch
were not the women already seated at our places, thE
reservoirs silos powder boxes packers seated,
they watch them, fill them and conducT
them to the country chapel. If possible I will go down
with them to the beach, just before the entry oF
Who makes the spirit quake with indescribable unduL
ations? Ah... WhO
Ah... The lover devastateD
HeR bare arms sway like a torche that waS
transformed brusquely into a partial machine
cathode oscillator==a base of spiraled light O
If she was not content to be discouraG
to discover her breasts each time tO
kiss me when I wake her from a full nap when I ar
ticulate with care an arrangement of legs a posturE
after her excuses
which could be my vein or else gold
mine, waste or inheritance in cart poorly blocked
?

après déjeuner, deux années après, alors qu'il avaiT
appris à l'arrière au front en selle à dé-
plier la bâche, à rêver: "est-il celui qu'iL
aurait voulu être un jour? Nulle part
et pendant un bon moment après un déjeuner pareiL
ne sont-elles pas déjà assises à nos places, leS
reservoirs silos poudriers emballeuses assises,
les regardent, les remplissent et les conduisE
nt à la chapelle rural. Si possible je les ferA
i descendre à la plage, just devant l'entrée dE
Qui fait tressaillir l'esprit d'indicibles onduL
ations? Ah… QuI
Ah… L'amante s'écroulanT
SeS bras nus roulent comme une torche qui sE
transformerait brusquement en une machine partiellE
d'oscillateur cathodique == un pied d'lampe spiralé O
Si elle ne se contentait pas de se découraG
d'se découvrir les seins à chaque occasion dE
m'embrasser quand je l'éveille en plein somme quand
j'ar
ticule avec soin un arrangement de jambs une posturE
après ses excuses
quelle pourrait être ma mine sinon de filoN
jaunissant, d'ordure ou d'héritage en carrosse mal calé
?

Madame, excuse the	grevious Elzevier, but
Thou hast no more for me	the environment, verdure
That I loved to sli	p into at day's end at
The encounter of yo	ur kindness, of your of
Clientele, by na	ture, bitter, crazed
Your enchan	tress hole, that seems to me
Must be reread	each time the wall loses
Its color. For	give what is in a book
But do not forget	never forget that I
"hunting their	breasts with his hands
And looking at them	with their eyes dark and
Evil, all their	company, Aurélien traits
The solder slip	ping since the skin favo-
ed this	attention that you must
Give to my letter	and
"madeup, would you smil	e today with a
grace so young?" Sten	dhal, in the best of
Times, defining a	porte-cochère,
Brings the saliva	just in time.
	sweet

Madame, pardon de l'	Elzevier funeste, mais
N'as plus pour moi	d'environnement, de verdure
Que j'aimais à gli	sser en fin de jour vers
La rencontre de vo	tre amabilité, de votre de
Clientèle, des genr	es, acides, des fureurs
Votre trou enchan	teur, celui qu'il me semble
Devoir relire à	chaque fois que le mur perd
Sa couleur. Par	don que ce soit dans un livre,
Mais n'oubliez pas,	n'oubliez jamais que je

"couraient de leurs   poitrines à ses mains
Tes et regardaient   de leurs yeux sombres et
Mauvais, tout l'   équipage, et Aurélien buriné
Les soudures gli   ssant de puis l'écorce favo-
riseraient cette   attention que vous devriez
Porter à ma lettre   e
"fard, tu nous sourira   is aujourd'hui avec une
grâce si jeune?" Sten   dhal, dans le meilleurs
Temps, précisant une   porte chochère,
Porte la salive   au   sommet de l'heure.
                 doux

lines, yellow mechanical shafts, totally overlooked one
who appears to poorly support beginnings of phras
everything converges to transfer a collusion, sub
tract non-nostalgic memory, one or two
divinity beautiful candi. saltimbanque,
the same perspective, with pel
vis without end and prospect
ive, strange track
of the 8
beyond the state of all
comprehension, I salute you
and I deliver to you my version
8 when thou art a basket, without
more linen than ivory, without more
canapé than ivorine, without more wing
than taught the chansons de geste. He enclos
ed turpitude exigence shovels rifles of men for
asses of troupes of women. He will not come again ...

voies, fûts mécaniques jaunes, par-dessus tout un
qui paraît supporter mal les entrées de phras
tout concourt à traduire une collusion, ot
e souvenir non nostalgique, un ou deu
ivinité belle candi. saltimbanque,
la même perspective, con pel
vis sans fin et prospect
tive, course étrange
du 8
hors de tout état de
compréhension, je vous sa
lue et je vous livre ma lectu
re. 8 quand tu es corbeille, sans
plus de linge que l'ivoire, sans plus
de canapé qu'ivoirine, sans plus d'aile qu
elle apprenait les chansons de geste. Il l'enf
erma turpitude exigence pelles fusils d'homme pour
les fesses de tourbe de femme. Il n'y paraîtra plus.….

Confronting *of the* 8, d'Assoucy remarks in 1677
"Why then, sex the color of rose..."

Here from this should be a very long poem
written almost 5 years ago and whose title (sole remaining
sum to me of the total) was made of a legend in a major state
of completion. Being 7 or 8 times longer than the
poem of the whirligig-man confronting the hourglass woman, this poem
will only subsist here as a "fingerprint". Perhaps
it may appear at the end of the work?

En face de *du* 8, d'Assoucy entonne en 1677:
"Pourquoi donc, sexe au teint de rose"…

Ici pourrait de même prendre place de très long poème écrit il ya près de 5 ans et dont le titre (seul souvenir net qui m'en reste) était fait d'une légende complète de carte d'état-major. Etant 7 ou 8 fois plus long que le *poème de l'homme-toupie en face de la femme-sablier,* ce poème ne subsistera ici que sous son "empreinte". Peut-être pourrait-il figurer en fin d'ouvrage?

Now the bath tub with the roe deer above
She would have known immediately what had to be
Done, that our walks had made a deli-
Cious scandal, had revealed the dream of foolish
emotions, capital offense to which we had no right
F   orce of loving that forces a lesson.
So   me thing agreeable to its own ironic fashion.
Lik   e there is no quarter and that we
Accep   t any of the least suitable spoiled
Vermin   with calluses, ––– nal fears
So versa   tile that exactly the bubons like
Mules   and like horses poorly placed on the tub
Beca   use they are totally up against the deer
That   is to say flank/flank, and that she
Os   cillates still, a good player in spite of

All   flow. *And*   says
   in the   *to win*, as
Crevel,   *where they*
   his desk   *find*
             ALCOOLS.

<u>Poem from an old passage from the "petit" Rhône</u>

Maintenant le bac avec les chevreuils dessus
Elle aurait su immédiatement ce qu'il y avait
A faire, que nos promenades ont fait le déli-
Cieux scandale, a révélé le rêve de sentiments
insensés, injure capital qu'on n'a pas le droit
F   orce de s'aimer ce qu'il faudrait la leçon.
Qu   elque chose d'aimable à sa façon d'ironiser,
Com   me il n'y avait pas de quartier et qu'on n'en
Accep   te aucun parmi les moins aptes dépouillées
Vermin   es à callositiés, ——— nales peurs
Si versa   tiles qu'exactement les bubons comme
Mulets   et comme chevaux mal placés sur le bac
Parce   qu'ils sont tout contre les chevreuils
Pour   ainsi dire flanc / flanc, et qu'elle
Os   cille encore, bonne joueuse malgré

Tout   courant. *Et*   dit
    dans le   *de gagner*, comme
Crevel,   *où se*
    son bureau   *trouvent les*   …
    ALCOOLS.

<u>*Poème d'un passage ancien du petit Rhône*</u>

He has not however the style to atte
Except to look at her, to— what the read
To recognize her, to whom begins to b
Bystanders in the opposite camp, v
Sewn in thy white thread of am
"Let us go then, this is onl
Very good to retell it, milli   **HIDDEN**
Of clothes distributed… we
Bad "to happen most in swal
Distance as far away as possib
Moment to leave again we are
Nope! To wear trousers on
Sumptuous hostess who looks, i
Colonial, farmer or master of the house la
Ass having greatly laughed. (Lexique, page 192 et sq like
Pleynet
"Hostess presiding leaning at the level where she can see that one no longer
Would catch her in the position of a reader of a boudoir poem.

Il n'a pourtant pas le genre à atte
Hors à la regarder, à — que le lec
La reconnaître, à qui vient d'êt
Passants dans le camp opposé, v
Cousu dans ton fil blanc d'am
"Allons donc, cela n'est qu'
Très bon d'en reparler, milli
De vêtements distribués...on
Mal "arriver le plus en aval
Distance au plus loin possib
Moment de repartir nous soyon
Tin! A porter une culotte sur
Somptueuse hôtesse qui regarde, i
Colon, fermier ou le maître de céans ri
Ane ayant beaucoup ri. (Lexique, page 192 et sq comme
Pleynet
"Hôtesse demeurant accoudée au niveau où elle peut voir qu'on ne l'y
Reprendrait plus en position de lectrice de poème couchée

CACHES

Eros, Lymne Cycle

Éros, cycle de Lymne

POEM IN THE FORM OF A CALLIGRAMME

The ancient plain, would testify that she
Determines the basis of what is going to be butter
And the content in water
In bad water, listening to the sink water, you have
Been carefully and sweetly controlled
The feet and the exquisite heat of the wheat without
Exception offering the harvest is here even religious
And material together, a joking matter and
Religious for peacemakers one would never interrupt
Except at the day and hour of the Ist casting
Of rules
The feet and the exquisite head of the grain without
$\qquad\qquad\qquad\qquad\qquad$ — I said —

Exception_____
And bending languishingly from one tomb to the other
"to fall into bondage and follow the country it-
self
To guard a void, but it's the proof, and
How, through what excess, in order to put them in
A spiritual center, judges, short story writers
The frightening chaos of a beautiful feminine evening.

POEME EN FORME DE CALLIGRAMME

L'ancienne plaine, serait témoigné qu'elle
Détermine le fond de ce qui va être le beurre
Et le contenu en eau
En mal d'eau, écoutant l'eau de plonge, tu as
Eté avec beaucoup de soin et doucement contrôlée
Les pieds et l'exquise chaleur du grain sans
Exception dont la cueillette est ici même culte
Et matière à la fois, matière à plaisanterie et
Culte pour pacificatrices qu'on n'interromprait
Jamais qu'au jour et à l'heure de la Iere coulée
De règles
Les pieds et l'exquise chaleur du grain sans
$\qquad$ — disais-je —

Exception_____
Et penche languissamment d'une tombe à l'autre
"tomber dans une esclave et suivre le pays lui-
même
Garder un vide, mais c'est la preuve, et
Comment, par quel excès, pour les mettre dans
Un centre de spiritueux, juges, nouvellistes
L'affreux chaos d'un beau soir feminine.

Only the narrative parts appear here strictly speaking. Rhyming couplets, the figures called "forked trees" will be integrated in another work. In every way, the present book is a first opportunity for me to no longer respect the chronological order of literary creation. First order then: read. The journey always follows some introductory discourse or some word order, even tacit.

Ne figurant ici que les parties de narration proprement dite. Les couplets versifiés, les figures dites "arbres fourchus" seront intégrés dans un autre ouvrage. De toute façon, le livre présent est un première occasion pour moi de ne plus respecter l'ordre chronologique de la création littéraire. Premier présent donc: lire. Les périples suivent toujours quelque discours d'introduction ou quelque mot d'ordre, même tacite.

Lymne dared not move: the captain staggered on
A black whale in order to recover there a cigarette
Ital. populat. from a local town, in the center of
An oscillation the segment attached to the shark axis
Particular (joyous female assistants) sharks on
Equal footing. But the glittering that spreads out
Puts a head in his penis plays now to cra-
Ckle like a blade of a grinder that fatigue kills.
Surely the cause of your impotency weak shales
And to believe women could hold in these fr-
Aile colors the tears that they shed and the
Lava flows they emit like trumpets…
Drenchings always more dark they follow me
In my first movement of love that makes me throw out
Very far the amusement of my first versions (under
stand: "the poem" or "the poems", if the
reshufflings in view of the definitive publication
do not hinder me from remembering exactly the number
of poems forming the Lymne Cycle) What does it matter?
Surprises, floods, they scratch each other out in the vapor

Lymne n'osait bouger: le capitaine titubait sur
Une baleine noire pour y retrouver une cigarette
Ital. populat. d'une commune, dans le centre d'
Une oscillation le segment attaché à l'axe requins
Particuliers (joueuses préparatrices) requins sur
Un pied d'égalité. Mais le brillant qui s'étale
Mis la tête dans sa queue jouait maintenant à cré-
Piter comme une pale de moulin que la fatigue tue.
Bien la cause de votre impuissance faibles marnes
Et de croire qu'elles pouvaient tenir dans ces fai-
Bles couleurs les larmes qu'elles versant et les
Laves qu'elles commettent comme trompettes...
Rincées toujours plus obscures elles vont me suivre
Dans mon premier mouvement d'amour qui me fait jeter
Fort loin l'amusement des premières versions (sous
entendu: "du poème" ou "des poèmes", puisque les
remainements en vue de la publication définitive
m'empèchent de me souvenir avec certitude du nombre
de poèmes formant le cycle de Lymne) Qu'importe.
Surprises, crues, elles se dévisagent dans la vapeur

They, the same, the hunt in supple form
And open, by liquored faith that uses
Hard widowhood to satisfy, to move the limits
From isle to isle of the rest of the irritated vamps.
A small garden. Enclosed? "Dust raised up" in
Fairy tales (Sister Anne, silky but-
Tucks Liliputian at the top of the tower spanks
Banners leading the cortege of lingerie and
My intense emotion singly breaks its back)
I take back, after "enclosed": What callousness
Powerfully dynamic can darken a
Bed at the instant of strongest emigrations, of
Most of them with poison of tig-

They advance in spite of the frosts following
Without diminishing watching making this woman who her
There is no royal ferment well off (or torment)
This fortification, I make a resolution to
Wash here what remains obviously for us to do
Irreproachably spattered on the drapes—
Providing that they follow their path
From the high terrace of the academic college

Ils, la même, la chasse en une forme souple
Et ouverte, par la foi liquoreuse qui l'emploie
Dur veuvage à remplir, à déplacer les limites
D'îlot à îlot des restes d'allumeuse irritée.
Jardinet? Enclos? "Poussière soulevée" dans
Les contes de fées (la soeur Anne, fesses so-
Yeuses liliputiennes en haut de la tour claque
Des bannières devant le cortège de lingerie et
Mon émoi tendu séparément à craquer vers son dos)
Je reprends, après "enclos": Quelle callosité
Puissamment dynamique se peut obscurcir un
Lit au moment des plus fortes émigrations, de
La plupart d'entre eux avec des poisons de tig-

Avancèrent malgré les gelées au temps suivant
Sans diminuer regarder faire cette femme qui se
Il n'est pas de royal ferment aisé (ou tourment)
Cette muraille, je prends la résolution d'y
Baigner ce qui'il nous reste de décidément fait
D'irréprochablement éparpillé sur les draps —
Pendant qu'elles sont à suivre leurs cours
Du haut des gradins du collège académique

Almost a hollow sound that also fell upon him
And over there, in the marketplace of the missing reading
Porters of terms or of messages of excellent
Wellbeing (that we would be disoriented by a term "well-
Being" is this testament of relations already passably
Obscure?)
Suddenly grown up, half in bloom, son to
Bend by a sudden clumsy or monkish judgement.
Less at this age, because it comes to an end.
These pigs frightened at the interior of the inner sanctum
This region of gold too rich for cunts too well endowed
—What is it (affluent context of inquest)
—Doubtless the same demands (simultaneous?)
In the hotel room, in the alleys
Behind which the women play their game, with him
Restless now for sole omission
That he is more and more like cured

Presque un vide-timbres qui est lui aussi tombé
Et par là, sur le marché du manque de lecture
Porteurs de termes ou de messages d'excellente
Santé (serions-nous dépaysés qu'un terme "san-
té" est témoin de relations déjà passablement
Obscurcies?)   il
Tout à coup qui grandit, arbre à demi, fils à
Plier par un soudain jugement malhabile ou moine.
Moins avec cet âge, puisqu'il vient à une fin.
Ces cochons effrayés à l'intérieur du cénacle
Cette région d'or trop cher à culs trop bénis
—Qu'est-ce que c'est (contexte aisé d'enquête)
—Sans doute les mêmes demandes (simultanées?)
Dans la chambre de l'hôtel, dans les allées
Derrière lesquelles elles ont dû jouer, lui
S'agite maintenant avec pour seule omission
Qu'il est de plus en plus comme corroyé

Love being the physical union of two beings
in order that the masses confound together, producing an
impulsion of atoms.

In *Pauliska* or modern perversity,
by Reveroni Saint-Cyr, in the year VI

L'amour étant l'union physique de deux êtres
pour que les masses se confondent, donnez l'impulsion aux
atomes.

in *Pauliska* ou la perversité moderne,
par Reveroni Saint-Cyr, an VI

"18. —PHOENICIAN. The air tenebrous, the spirit of the air
tenebrous and chaos, these are the first principles of
the universe.

They are infinite, and they existed for a long time
before any limit circumscribed them.

But the spirit animates these principles: the stirring
begins, things unite, love is born and the
world begins.

The spirit does not at all comprehend its generation.

The spirit uniting all things engenders *word*.

Word according to some is primal clay, according
to others the putrefaction of a watery mass...

After the production of the *word*, follows the creation of
the sun,
the moon and the other stars."

1803.

"18. — PHENICIENNE. L'air ténébreux, l'esprit de l'air ténébreux et le chaos, sont les principes premiers de l'universe.

Ils étaient infinis, et ils ont existé longtemps avant qu'aucune limite les circonscrivit.

Mais l'esprit anima ses principes: le mélange se fit, les choses se lièrent, l'amour naquit et le monde commença.

L'esprit ne connut point sa génération.

L'esprit liant les choses engendra *mot*.

Mot est selon quelques-uns le limon; selon d'autres la putréfaction d'une masse aqueuse…

Après la production du *mot*, suivit celle du soleil, de la lune et des autres astres."

1803.

I seek the place where thy gown flaps
The foundations now revealed for a
New hunt, more could even be accomplished
If each holds to his own plan. "Pier"
Selling salted brochettes underwear commerce for
Peruvian women, and beneath two large rimon—
2 large concentric wheels ()
That are going to pucker up on the enormous neck of the
Good God, he no longer needs it; the achievements are
Loaded with the arms of men who guard the premises of the factory
Rake in hand, of my supple approach, breathing
Rant presently with great force, but quiet
I head for the Eden of iniquity, raised,
The passage that ends at the bottom of its three steps
Still appears to me of a rose insufficient in order that
Thy calves so poorly sheathed with silk do not shine there
With too many immodest desires, tamed by his hands
By him with his poised billiard cue and his cards

Je recherche l'endroit où ta robe frappe
Les fondations maintenant relevées pour une
Nouvelle chasse, même plus pourrait être accompli
Si chacun s'en tenait au plan qu'il possède. "Pier"'
Vendant brochettes salées enterprises à culottes pour
Péruviennes, et en dessous deux grandes rimon——
2 grandes roues concentriques ()
Qui viennent se plisser contre le cou démesuré du
Bon Dieu, il n'en faut pas plus; les réussites sont
Chargées à bras d'homme à qui garde les locaux d'l'usine
Râteau en main, de ma démarche souple, respirant
Rant à présent avec une grande force, mais tranquille
Je me dirige vers l'Eden d'iniquité, surélevé,
L'allée qui finit au bas de ses trois marches
Me paraît encore d'un rose insuffisant pour que
Tes mollets si mal gainés de soie n'y brillent
Trop d'immodestes désires; approvoisée de ses mains
A lui de son billard lové et de ses cartes

After lunch two years after when he had
Learned at the rear. Had spread out the tarp, had dreamed
Is he the one he would have wanted to be one day?
Nulle and for a good while, after a simi-
Lar lunch. Are they not already seated at
Our places, the gas tank had been filled
And to drive them to the village chapel, if pos-
Sible to make them descend to the place, just
Before the entry, which makes the spirit tremble
With unspeakable undulations. "Ah" the lover destroying
His naked arms, rumblings of illiterates, whom I
Mock, if she was not content her
Self to bare her breasts when I awake her before
Catching a nap. "Good, and then?" After her
Excuses what could be my mien other than some
Cushy fartslingers or even bitter crap?

Après déjeuner deux ans après alors qu'il avait
Appris à l'arriere. A déplié la bâche, a rêvé
Est-il celui qu'il aurait voulu être un jour?
Nulle et pendant un bon moment, après un déjeu-
Ner pareil. Ne sont-elles pas déjà assises à
Nos places, le réservoir d'essence a été rempli
Et les conduire à la chapelle du village, si pos-
Sible les faire descendre sur la place, juste
Devant l'entrée, qui fait tressaillier l'esprit
D'indiciples ondulations. "Ah" l'amante s'écroulant
Ses bras nus, roulements d'illettrés, dont je me
Moque, si elle ne se contentait pas de se
Découvrir les seins quand je l'éveille avant de
Repiquer un somme. "Bon, et alors?" Après ses
Excuses quelle pourrait être ma mine sinon de
Filons pétaradeurs ou même d'ordures aigres?

        as he had to give a title, to this
poem that did not turn out to be long and had been
completely redone three times, it was FLOWER, HEAT.
I always take this position before the machine—hard
ly brushed by the wind that sweeps towards the line
of the plum panels half up the hillside and under the sun
as if he were only above me
And FLOWER, HEAT

in order to finish they were telephoned to appear with ink
the day after tomorrow

       you pass now to the reading of FLOWER, HEAT
                                                      that
ought to find in regard to these words, at least that some
imperatives of fabrication had not "re-employed" them as
                                            say
the archaeologists on the verso of this page. If that were,
you have the complacency to return in the rear. We believe we
dream that we play at the game of the goose.

      comme il avait bien fallu lui donner un titre, à ce
poème qui n'en finissait pas d'être long et d'avoir été
entièrement refait trois fois, ce fut FLEUR, CHALEUR.
J'occupe toujours cette position devant la machine— à
peine effleuré par le vent qui s'engouffrait vers l'arête
du vantail en plein mi-coteau de colline et sous le soleil
comme s'il n'était au-dessus que de moi.
Et FLEUR, CHALEUR

pour finir leur fut téléphoné pour paraître avec l'encre
un surledemain

    passez maintenant à la lecture de FLEUR, CHALEUR
                              qui
devrait se trouver en regard de ces mots, à moins que des
impératives de fabrication ne l'aient "remployé" comme
                              disent
les archéologues au verso de cette page. Si cela était, ayez
l'obligeance de revenir en arrière. On croit rêver qu'on
joue au jeu de l'oie.

1798.

> From an old flask of usquebac
> That I guzzled long ago, I still snort the dregs;
> > Being broke, with plates of brass,
> > > My frugal fare serves life.
>
> Evening and morning, in my sorry port- sack,
> Carefully I wrap crust and dough;
> > I make my dessert a forgotten oublie.
> With my furry friends I no longer follow the track.
> In my cinch, O Time, you no more make me tic tock;
> and so on and so forth pimp,
> > > shame.
>
> > > clac,
> > > mania,
> > > fac.

1798.

> *D'un ancien flacon de*   scubac
> *Que je flûtais jadis, je flaire encor la*   lie;
> *Faute d'argent, en couverts de*   tombac,
> *Ma table frugale est ser*   vie.

> *Soir et matin, dans mon triste havre-*   sac,
> *Soigneusement j'enferme croûte et*   mie;
> *Je fais mon dessert d'une*   oublie.
De mes cheveux aimés je n'entends plus le   trac.
Dans ma ceinture, ô temps, tu ne fais plus tic   tac;
et ainsi de suite   mac,
                                                        humilie.

                                                        clac,
                                                        manie,
                                                        fac.

FLOWER, HEAT.

Not the first ones to carry from short build-
Ings, fires extinguished, all terrific, it is
Both immoral fort without inhabitants, immoral small fort
Without Americanism without lesson without hibiscus but
Only conceived for lips that would be very dirty.
Here remains some good springtime (I mean
That it appears to us "good" given our mi-
Serable situation little overcome)...
For thee of course the abiding sawmill with its common
Odor, with its feigned yellow evaporation, like the
Season that dreams of dryness ("ah, ravishing flourishes"
There where women would only be a beginning
Like birds, or flowers that we plant
From water layer on water layer, from rice pudding on
Rice pudding) the little adobe fort calcifies, in
This insupportable heat. Harder and harder,
It becomes a cosy building, with the florist
—and the merchant of English clockworks whose thread
In Needle is much more expensive than the gorm—

For us the rust infers as well the
Essence of thy forest as the full outcry of the orvet
That she not go to the vicinal sawmill that kills.

FLEUR, CHALEUR.

Ne pas les premiers à porter de courts immeu-
Bles, feux éteints, tous des fortiches, c'est à la
Fois l'immoral fort sans habitants, l'immoral fortin
Sans américanisme sans leçon sans hibiscus mais seu-
Lement conçu pour des lèvres qui seraient très sales.
Ici demeure quelque printemps bien (je veux dire
qui'il nous paraît "bien" étant donné ce que notre si-
Tuition a de misérable et de peu conquérant)…
A toi bien sûr la scierie demeurant de son ordinaire
Odeur, de sa feinte évaporation jaune, comme la
Saison qui rêve au sec ("ah, fioritures ravies"
Là où elles ne devraient être qu'un commencement
Comme les oiseaux, ou les fleurs qu'on repique
De nappe d'eau en nappe d'eau, de riz au lait en
Riz au lait) le fortin d'adobe se calte, avec
Cette chaleur insupportable. De dur en dur,
Il deviant l'immeuble cossu, avec le fleuriste
—et le marchand de rouages anglais quide fil
En Aiguille coûte bien plus cher que le gorm—

Pour nous la rouille devine aussi bien les
Essences de ta forêt que l'ample clameur d'orvet
Qu'elle n'aille pas à la scie vicinale qui tue.

Between poetry and rhetoric there is but one difference: poetry, taking as sufficient the variety of its forms, is succinct and obscure; rhetoric, basking in its humorous aspect and, by its rhythmic measure and veritably splendid meters, its feet, its accents, its tones and syllables, consolidates its grandeur and its beauty.

VIth century

Entre la poésie et la rhétorique il y a une différence: la poésie, tenant pour suffisante la variété de ses formes, est resserrée et obscure; la rhétorique, elle, se complaît dans son aspect riant et, par son compte rhythmique véritablement splendide de mètres, de pieds, d'accents, de tons et de syllabes, elle consolide son ampleur et sa beauté.

VIe siècle

I descended to this cabin whose
Age was rather indicative of a slight hillyness
Towards thy domain thy red neck of the corner of the domain
That stretches out before me, rays more blue more direct
"And to send us, windblown across undula-
ting waters and spilled drinks" towards (again)
The mute axles of vines! There is the landscape!
"Vigny and Rimbaud drink" since the question here
would be about them in these "lines"
My guests are responsible for the butter, and melancho-
Ly in order to return to it like a Sorrento wood factory
And some residue of bed linen
Tempted to write more than sea air is to a
False nut. And from my interior she cries and
Rushes to her pursuit. "Consummate murderers, flat on
Your stomach, fuck you!" The mistake is that it is of the
Wind…

Je suis descendu dans cette cabine dont
L'époque était assez indicatrice d'un collinement lêger
Vers ton domaine ton cou rouge du coin du domaine
Qui devant moi s'allonge, rayons plus bleus plus carrês
"Et nous envoyer, fouettêes à travers les eaux clapo-
tantes et les boissons répandues" vers (encore)
Les muets essieux des vignes! Le voilà le paysage!
"Vigny et Rimbaud boivent" puisque c'est d'eux qu'il
pourrait être question ici dans ces "lignes"
Mes invités comptent pour du beurre, et la mélanco-
lie pour en revenir comme d'une fabrique de sorrentes
Et des résidus de literie
Tenté d'écrire plus que ne l'est de l'air marin un
Ecrou de faux. Et dans mon intérieur elle crie et
Se jette à sa poursuite. "Tueuses consommées, à plat
Ventre, couchez-vous!" Le tort c'est que c'est du
Vent…

But oppressed by the weight of a lie pain terror
The course of this perilous interview "if you please
Monsieur" Night fallen, I kiss on the lips a pos-
A milkmaid, not finding herself wounded with sentiments
As much as she could but unguarded she will abuse the
Hedges, there is nothing that I am able to do that she
Has not already combatted: body that rests, lapses rested
Thou are but the body of the parabola, thy melon of fe-
Male geometry makes its own position, thy penchant
For the alienated lover of the tree will find waiting and
Prepared. Agreed upon this point, thy apartment,
—permission to wall up _____ In vain
I defend myself against the apprehension of the art of my
                                  writing, writing, writing

Mais oppressé du poids d'un mensonge peine terreur
Le cours de cet entretien périlleux "s'il vous plaît
Monsieur" La nuit tombée, je baise aux lèvres une pos-
Une laitière, ne se trouve blessé dans les sentiments
Autant qu'elle peut mais par mégarde elle abusera des
Haies, il n'y a rien que je ne puisse y faire qu'elle
N'ait déjà combattu: corps qui repose, oublis reposés
Tu n'es que le corps de la parabole, ton melon de fem-
Me géomètre se fait à son emplacement, ton penchant
Pour l'amant aliéné de l'arbre trouvera pâte et
Couchant. D'accord sur ce point, ton appartement,
—permission de murer _____ En vain
Je me défends contre l'appréhension de l'art de mon
                    écriture, écriture, écriture

The Library of Congress

La bibliothèque du congrès

I have been a word among letters.

V^th century

J'ai été mot parmi les letters.

Ve siècle.

More breath even, hardly under the pain of—mounds or
In mountains, those that are original—the
Concentration in men of the village, until
Our era furnishing the exile in the woods
Not the present, not in August 1762
This complacent victual, the indifference to the
Laws of the hunt on the terrain, or of the cou-
Sin she who had the right to hunt in the fields
And the plums like a pain or a triumph
And they return every evening to the village, loose as-
Pect of pastoral ardor, of protective
Thatch, if he was happy with the service of the
Thatch. Between stories and the soul of
Profound voices. The custom, in the forest, of their own
Thing.

Plus même l'haleine, sous à peine des—monts ou
En montagnes, celles qui sont originelles—la
Concentration en hommes de la commune, jusqu'à
Nos jours fournissant le dépaysement aux bois.
N'est pas le présent, n'est pas en août 1762
Cette victuaille complaisante, la froideur des
Droits de chasse sur le terrain, ou de la cou-
Sine qui avait le droit de chasse sur les terres
Et les pruneaux comme une peine ou un triomphe
Et rentraient tous les soirs au village; l'as-
Pect desserré des fougues pastorales, de chaume.
Protégeant, s'il était content du service des
Chaumes. Entre les nouvelles et l'ame des voix
Profondes. L'usage, en forêt, de leur proper
Chose.

At the foot of the post of his hollow countenance, and
He himself asking where to rest his fatigue,
She had the counterweight in a weak secretion
The joys of friendship in my city, naked
Like the objective, with harvests and bonfire
In short with my absence at these earth tremors.
Under the pretext that we are far from them, is it not
So? The olive breast beating the wood or the water
If it is there that the ordinary stone rolls
The orgasm like a wink after the crocodile
The tea on the place of the mining displaces the wind
The traffic on the road, storehouse of ore
Finds itself disturbed by the sum of a hundred beasts
That go to the forge with the six merchants; in
Modest warehouses; the fear of not coming
Or of not coming again under the same visages.

Au pied du poteau de sa mine creuse, et
Lui-même à se démander où asseoir sa fatigue,
Elle avait le contre-poids dans un sanie faible
Les joies de l'amitié dans ma ville, nues
Comme à l'objectif, avec les moissons et le feu
Bref de mon absence à ces roulements par terre.
Sous prétexte qu'on est loin d'eux, n'est-ce
Pas? La poitrine olive battant le bois ou l'eau
Si c'est là que l'ordinaire caillou fait bouler
L'orgasme comme un cil après le crocodile.
Le thé sur la place du minier déplace le vent.
Le trafic sur la route, entrepôts de minerai se
Trouvaient inquiets de la somme des cent bêtes
Qui vont à la forge avec les six marchands; en
Trepôts modestes: la crainte de pas faire venir
Ou de pas faire revenir sous les mêmes visages.

thought, we guess that it is some case of
Noblesse (like there above the earth blocking
The night owls looking at them under their nose with a
Crown colored with seagull shit) with me they see
Again this activity of ten years ago, especially those
Of the wilderness, in large part the ideal more or
Less accessible to the intelligence that animates it.
Servant of the knot of the sacred thought… they only
Survived, this drop just beneath the lip that
She will only give back to him tomorrow, having sprayed
The baths of the village
that she is not accessible in the archaism
Neither her lack of point of view of my con-
Tact, under the mountain man who would have a constant
Drive. Of these last, 16 only
Precarious.

pensée, nous estimons qu'il est des cas par
Noblesse (comme là au-dessus de la terre contrant
Les chevêches en les regardant sous le nez avec un
Pic coloré d'ordure de mouette) avec moi ils re-
Voient cette activité d'il y a dix ans, surtout ceux
De la friche, en grande partie l'idéal plus ou
Moins accessible à l'intelligence qui l'animait.
Serviteur du noeud de la pensée sacreé… n'ont
Survécu, cette goutte juste sous la lèvre qu'
Elle ne lui redondera que demain, ayant pluvérisé
Les bains du village
qu'elle n'est pas accessible dans l'archaïsme
Ni son manque au point de vue de mon con-
Tact, sous le montagnard qui aurait un constant
Entraînement. Sur ces derniers, 16 seulement
Précaires.

is not permitted to hide capital and speculate
On large purchases. "For Catalan iron which
Was valued at 435 F in 1840, did not exceed… etc."
tière of man is a revelation of this good.
He would miss the bed or the quarry and then God.
Because the deep repulsion is like a
City that thou hast set against another that for him
Had made nothing but that would feature well the same
Silk as the illustrious gown. This I remove from you
That one honors profane grace, the
Perfume of thy cloth without a hint of the sheepfold.
The perfume of thy beverage that evaporates in the sun
I dare not say naked and empty if she is
Posed at this instant other than at
The window, or the marble of the washbasin, or the
Thick flowery grass he pushes her towards?

est pas permis d'effacer capitaux et spéculent
Sur les gros achats. "Or les fers catalans qui
Valaient 435 F vers 1840, ne dépassent… etc."
tière de l'homme est une rèvèlation de ce bon.
Il manquerait le lit ou la proie et puis Dieu.
Parce que la répulsion profonde c'est comme une
Ville que tu as jetée contre l'autre qui ne lui
Avait rien fait mais qui arborait bien la même
Soierie que l'illustre robe. Cella-là je t'l'ôte
Celle-la met en honneur la grâce profanée, le
Parfum de ton linge sans l'ombre de la bergerie.
Le parfum de ton breuvage qui s'évapore au soleil
Je n'ose pas dire nue et vide si elle s'est
Posée a cette heure autrement qu'au travers de
La vitre, ou du marbre du lavabo, ou de la
Fleur grasse vers laquelle il la pousse?

The degradation strictly localized (I
Return to the s, because I hold them in
My image as well as the gross dazzling heart
On the butcher's block. Ho Jerusalem!) constituting
The essential element of the activity of my language,
Better that you have not divulged our weaknesses,
To show and prostrate ourselves to impetuosity, the
Banner "Grace" could be blue like the
Asparagus of Mount Carnivore, or better that which I
Imagine somewhere in a grave
Of dust and amnesty, of friendship. Coots
You might hear again, if you needed it,
But what fish from hell that we no longer use,
That you would no more come to harvest with
Your frightening wax fingers, on the bed.

L'avilissement strictement localisé (je
Reviens sur le s, parce que je les tiens dans
Mon image aussi bien que le gros coeur clinquant
Sur le billot. Hein Jerusalem!) constituant
L'élément essentiel de l'activité de ma langue;
Mieux que vous n'avez dévoilé nos faiblesses,
Monter et se prosterner dans l'impétuosité, le
Fanion "Miséricorde" pourrirait de bleu comme l'
Asperge du mont Carnivore, ou bien celui que je
Devinerai quelque part dans un ensevelissement
De poussière et d'amnistie, d'amitié. Foulques
T'entendrais-tu à nouveau, s'il te le fallait,
Mais que de poissons en enfer que nous ne salerions
Plus, que tu ne viendrais plus recueillir dans
Tes doigts de cire épouvantables, sur le lit.

where are the fauve babies going, at least the first at the
Front, the treasurer's award to the new arrival in
Pieces, like "piece of cloth" or like system
Of irrigation "for the buffoons", the danger of
Foraging during the night for fodder.
Specially that my regard does not cross thy field from isle
To isle pursuing a long march/brands on ani-
Mals, memories of shoes without marks, etc
At the moment where disaffection comprises a basic faci-
Lity that I use in winter at the moment.
What is better, cabins fitted with vigor-
Ous scatterbrains, cleaning women for boyards or
Bacchanales of the modern epic with splendors in the fore
That I no longer be interested in some congress
That this be, some field of fatal idea
That this be

où vont les bébés fauves, du moins les chefs de
File, la trésorière donnée à l'arrivant par
Pièces, comme "pièce de drap" ou comme pièce
D'arrosage "pour les bateleurs"; le danger de
La circulation pendant la nuit pour le fourrage.
Surtout que mon regard ne croise ton field d'île
En île poursuivant une randonnée/marques de bê-
Tes, souvenirs de souliers sans taches, etc
Au moment où l'éloignement comporte une install-
Lation sommaire que j'utilise en hiver au moment.
Ce qui'il y a de mieux, cabanes munies de vigou-
Reuses écervelées, nettoyeuses de boyards ou
Bacchantes de l'épopée moderne des lustres avant
Que je ne sois plus intéressé par quelque congrès
Que ce soit, quelque plaine de néfaste idée
Que ce soit.

bestial all acts of kindness, for the advo-
She the one. —howls and this relentless succession of
Very devious men, the particularly clever fact
Of their spreading, through my own view
Of their arms, or of their going, and coming with
The idea of a rogation (to right or to left,
Putting down their fistful of copious hair,
Eager for coronations that come and go
with …) and south of these 120 cows that I had
The pleasure to see, between the trips over these
Estates, concession to the winter deliveries,
Coming much less from the allure of the plainsman
She here where the lavatory apes the apse. She
Is pinned up like a gaiter, and, I
Who placed the pins, I wait for her.

bestiaux sur tous les bienfaits, sur l'avo-
Celle. —raires et cette succession continue d'
Hommes bien intrigants, le fait particulièrement
Net de leur étendue, à travers ma proper vue
De leurs armes, ou de leur allée, et venue dans
L'idée d'une rogation (à droite ou à gauche,
Couchant leur poignée de chevelure à foison,
Empressés des couronnements qui vont et viennent
à…) et dans le sud de ces 120 vaches que j'ai
Du plaisir à regarder, entre les parcours de ces
Domaines, concession des arrivages hivernaux,
Proviennent bien moins des allures d'homme de plaine
Celle-ci où le lavatory singe l'abside. Elle
Est clouée dessus comme une guêtre, et, moi
Qui ai mis les clous, je l'attends.

That the work traveled the streets resounding
Widely in order to satisfy the course, the com-
Munity (it is true that one of them
Knew what combat, and at what speed, with
A chambermaid whom she ruined and who died from
Seeing her) Sniff the resin high up, what
Reparian restraint, and what mud that would tire thee
More than her legs and her parturitioning
Half spilled at that point, since he must
Help her get up and climb up to the first
House, while you catch your breath and
Sit down. He missed nightly this charac-
Ter, indocile, reigned an economy in part
But in part only, never with a bla-
Ze, of eleven hundred physical education instructors.

Que le travail a parcouru les rues en sonnant
Vastes pour suffire au parcours, sur les com-
Munaux (il est vrai qu'il en existait une qui
Avait su quel combat, et à quelle vitesse, à
Une chambrière qu'elle écorna et qui décéda de
La voir) Renifle la résine là-haut, quelle
Lacustre étreinte, et quelle boue qui t'aurait
Fatiguée plus que ses jambes et sa parturiente
A demi versée jusque-là, puisqu'il devait l'
Aider à se relever et monter jusqu'à la première
Maison, pendant que tu reprends haleine et
T'assieds. Il lui manqué nuitamment ce carac-
Tère, indocile, régnait une économie en partie
Mais en partie seulement, jamais avec un in-
Cendie, des mille et cent maîtres de gymnastique.

The beautiful season, the bills of lading of the
Kind; but what, that of weak tinctures.
Who had misconceived the conditions of libe-
... A partial settlement to assure the
Community, and then to walk tranquilly with
Her hanging onto my arms, towards the farm in order to
Buy a pullet, and then to come again, as if
To love her was not enough, nothing that may be, that
Could be sufficient in whatever that might be;
How alluring she is and what vertiginous soli-
Tude. There where I guard the evening. That we knew
But what would be best is not our
Dance, or the sweat that she would wipe at the place
And time of my death. I crown her a
Figure of the shepherd with rose water, in the talus
In th'talus.

La belle saison, les connaissements de la
Sorte; mais quoi, que de faibles teintures.
Qui avait méconnu les conditions de la libe-
… Une parcelle d'arrangement pour assurer le
Commun, et alors marcher tranquillement avec
Elle pendue à mes bras, vers la ferme pour
Acheter un poulet, et puis revenir, comme si
De l'aimer n'avait pas suffi, rien qui soit, qui
Puisse être suffisant en quoi que ce soit;
Qu'elle ait l'allure et la vertigineuse soli-
Tude. Là où je monte le soir. Qu'on a compris,
Mais ce qui serait le mieux n'est pas notre
Danse, ou la sueur qu'elle essuierait au lieu
Et à la date de ma mort. Je lui couronne une
Figure de pâtre à l'eau de rose, dans le talus
Dans l'talus.

basically, existence is concerned with the hayloft,
or rather with how she can come with my
Joy, with my erection of catholic eater,
"remains of the old world, young, strong, free…"
While he understands the neighbor lady with large grain
Like the house and, alone, he obscures
His design, wanting to travel no more than it's
Worth, than arrogance, then she
Makes it with an older guy, with the principal
House where she forcefully banishes the
Last ones from the house (from the bedroom rather)
                I read the path, with
The walls, like a cordial before dinner
Progressive, one who is going to rustle the cattle
Through the rotten country, the substantives girding
Thy brow with frost and deceit, me I
Eat the hot berry that aggravates each of thy
Steps.

en gros, l'existence intéressée avec le fenil,
ou plutôt par où elle peut venir à ma
Joie, à mon érection de mangeur catholique.
"restes du vieux monde, jeune, fort, libre…"
Lorsqu'il entend la voisine du grain grand
Comme la maison et, solitaire, il obscurcit
Son dessein, voulant ne voyager plus que de
Peines, plus que d'arrogance, alors elle se
Fait à un type plus ancien, avec la maison
Principale où elle se fait fort d'éloigner les
Derniers de la maison (de la chambre plutôt)
          Je lis le chemin, avec
Les murs, comme cordial d'avant dîner.
Progressiste, qui vas cueillir le bétail
Par le pays pourri, les substantifs ceignant
Ton front de gelées et de fraudes, moi je
Mange la baie chaude qu'irrite chacun de tes
Pas.

force of the forest but she would return with half
She comes closer with the basin without mani-
Festation of any kind or this some thing
Very fresh when afterwards, but how
This what hope to separate thus these breasts
So apparently flourishing with health?
From the city we perceive only this manner
Of enclosing, where the slant by which to penetrate there
Arranges the member, remounts her cush-
Ions, and then we can confirm the precision
Of the result and that the series complete with combi-
Nations to discover does not exceed the fantasy
That I must bestride you at least for the
Sensation that we think of the same thing in our dreams.

tire du bois mais elle retournait à demi
Elle se rapproche avec la cuvette sans mani-
Festation d'aucune sorte ou ce quelque chose
De très frais quand ensuite, mais comment
Cela quel espoir à séparer ainsi ces seins
D'une santé si apparemment florissante?
De la ville on aperçoit seulement cette manière
D'enveloppe, où le biais par lequel y pénétrer
Dispose l'équipier, se remonte sur ses cous-
Sins, et alors on peut constater l'exactitude
Du résultat et que la série complète des combi-
Naisons à découvrir n'excède pas la fantaisie
Que je devrai t'enjamber au moins pour la
Sensation que nous pensons à une chose en rêve.

Half-turn and of others themselves lost in bath-
Ing simply the second part of their body
Of their breasts with slick and frequent scents
Down to their feet of pre-caprine flesh color that makes
Them swallow the fish between two stones?
Who grants them the permission to restrain themselves
In a purse so narrow that they are not at all
Even comfortable to rub down the thorax or
To scratch the back of a friend? You see
The pine tree laying in its shroud, octagonal by dint
Of intrusions suffered and lips that one must de-
Cap with everything becoming heavy, muscular or…
The rocking of the road is electric or
The dust of the road or the rails cannot
Rise because it is too humid and that
Everything sticks as is not
Permitted.

Demi-tour et d'autres se sont perdues en bai-
Gnant simplement la deuxième partie de leur corps
De leurs seins d'habiles et fréquentes odorantes
Jusqu'a leurs pieds de race pré-caprine qui fait
Qu'elles noient le poisson entre deux cailloux?
Qui leur octroie la permission de se contraindre
En une bourse si étroite qu'elles n'y sont point
Même à l'aise pour se frictionner le thorax ou
S'y faire gratter le dos par une voisine? Voyez
Le pin couché dans son suaire, octogonal à force
D'intrusions subites et de lèvres qu'il faut dé-
Coiffer à toute venante alourdie, musclée ou…
Le balancement de la route se fait électrique ou
La poussière des voies ou des rails ne peut pas
S'élever à cause qu'il fait trop humide et que
Toutes les choses collent comme il n'est pas
Permis.

Ah! God! There then was the be-
st that with my fingertips I wanted
To match the gentleness of her moans. In a veritable
Apotheosis of the greatest joy of her life!
And like blood pulses to tell that it is breaking.
an incredible swiftness two Prussian cavaliers
and from *here the count* to *takes a basket* everything
is barred. The little seat with thy twin gums opens
To desire, a pale desire like venereal wind double
Beaked with inherited ugly members. And I wish by
This gentle slope to easily win the field on
The other side of the canal. Nothing does it for, aided
By a reverse, in this amiable moment, exhausted,
I see myself like a thieving peasant plucking
His heart in the filthy earth, and as
Swinburne says *what trace remains an hour
afterwards?*

Ah! Dieu! Que là était donc le meil-
leur dont du bout des doigts je voulais
Egaler la douceur du pleur. En une véritable
Apothéose de la plus grande joie de sa vie!
Et comme le sang démarre dire qu'il se brise.
une rapidité incroyable deux cavaliers prussiens
et depuis *ici le comte* jusqu'à *prit un panier* tout
est barré. Le tabouret à ta double gencive éclore
Vouloir, un vouloir pâle comme vent vénérien double
Bec à hériter d'amers members. Et je voudrai par
Cette pente douce gagner facilement le champ de
L'autre côté du canal. Rien n'y fit car, s'aidant
D'une renverse, dans cet amical moment, fourbu,
Je me vois ressembler à un paysan volant triant
Son coeur dans la terre dégueulasse, et comme dit
Swinburne *quelle trace en reste-t-il il y a une
heure?*

He saw nothing at all and, far from being overwhelmed by this, he made this absence of vision his culminating point of view.

M. Blanchot, 1948?

Il ne voyait rien et, loin d'en être accablé, il faisait de cette absence de vision le point culminant de son regard.

M. Blanchot, 1948?

We are only happy when doing it: this is my morality.

Mme Quinquet, an VII

On n'est heureux qu'en en faisant: c'est ma morale.

Mme Quinquet, an VII

.

I am not so sure of my minor desire
Her body after this fatigue a battle so
For what reasons if this was not because
"who? For what?... Ah!..." said Strind-
body after so many battles she gave the
Impression of sleep and my phrases are
Only restorations. Is it not so? And, when
Vines, fields, woods and all adjoining
Am, at an arched window MY WORDS LIKE
MESSENGERS PUT TO BED MY THOUGHT.
In fact I have come to look upon Blanchot
Like a bed of Voltairien clay, Pigal'
Le, you were a genius, I operate the pump
In the garden and the herbs converge at full
Steam towards the secretary of vaccinating needles
"the south side looks out upon the cemeteries and on
A staircase with numerous stairs separated
Into three stages"

Je ne suis pas si sûre de mon envie minime
Son corps après cette fatigue une lutte si
Pour quelles raisons si ce n'était à cause
"qui? Pour quoi?... Ah!..." disait Strind-
corps après tant de luttes elle donnait l'
Impression du sommeil et mes phrases ne sont
Que restaurations. N'est-ce pas? Et, cum
Vineis, campis, silvis et omnibus adjacentiis
Suis, à une fenêtre cintrée MES MOTS COMME
COURRIERS FONT AU LIT MA PENSÉE.
En fait je puis obtenir de regarder Blanchot
Comme d'un lit d'argile voltairienne, Pigal'
le, tu avais du génie, j'actionne la pompe
Du jardin et les herbes convergent à toute
Vapeur vers le secrétaire aux vaccinostyles
"le côté sud donne sur les cimetières et sur
L'escalier aux nombreuses marches coupées
Par trois paliers"

Iambics of Disaffection

Iambes de l'éloignement

The caressing cry of dogs in Homer.

André Chenier

Le cri caressant des chiens dans Homère.

André Chenier

Enve
Loped in her cloak which is a bathtub
    For who would take the words with
His fingers to lick in vain her two hands so rigid
    Thy rolling twists I was going myself
Like the narrow glove that strung the frost/
    The sorrowful tribe that the entire courtyard
Fills thinks that the broken chain could
Reweld itself (Alfieri)
I say, me, I ferret out everywhere in order that she
    Removing hat and provisions
Knows finally that she is full of tight discharges
    And that, will we be gallops and
Soap, all sadness is scorched and enclosed
    Nutritive undressed
Worn out villager == periodically at Limoux
            (lower Languedoc)
Thou—exposed vagina—Italy!

Enve
Loppée de sa cape qui est une baignoire
    Pour qui prendrait les mots avec
Ses doigts lécher en vain ses deux mains si rigides
    Tu roulant torsades m'irais
Comme l'étroit gant qui ficelait le givre/
    La triste gent dont toute cour
Est pleine pense que la chaîne rompue pour-
Ra se ressouder (Alfieri)
Je dirai, moi, je furetai partout pour qu'elle
    Otant chapeaux et fournitures
Sache enfin qu'elle est pleine d'étroites décharges
    Et que, serions-nous galops et
Savons, toute tristesse est cuite et renfermée
    Nourricière dévêtue
Villageoise élimée == périodique à Limoux
        (bas Languedoc)
Tu——le ventre à l'air——Italie!

The word having produced the nettle of lyricism!
Found greatly lacking when the wing falters
   In vain our lyric chasubles
Would blow the dust sentimentally
   The lady friend of the lyre crouches
Descending the satiated Helicon, repudiated.
   Fucking the suckling stranger
I follow them in the scope of my rifle
   Dreaming of piled up verses.

"Father editor in chief
with the broken head, my stones were they
   so gouty, sitted more curdled
than polders and my village then long piglets
   Bone calcium of the face and of caterpillars
Capturing in the race some Minotaur
   Too inflamed but credulous
He who eats virgins and ruins, cheeses"

Le verbe ayant produit l'ortie du lyrisme!
Se trouva fort dépourvu quand l'aile flancha
    En vain nos chasubles lyriques
En souffletaient-elles la poussière eau de rose
    L'amie d'la lyre s'accroupit
Descendant l'Helicon repue, répudiée.
    Baisant l'étrangère aux seins
Je les suis dans la lunette de mon fusil
    Rêvant de vers empilés:

"Père rédacteur en chef
à la tête cassée, mes cailloux étaient-ils
    si podagres, assis plus caillasses
que polders et mes village donc longs gorets
    Cal du visage et des chenilles
Attrapant à la course quelque minotaure
    Trop enflammé mais crédule
Celui qui mangeait vierges et ruines, fromages"

Elementary Eros always a Little Near October

Éros Élémentaire Toujours a Peu Près Octobre

The claw of the man who, feeling himself observed,
Lifts brusquely an elbow in the direction
Of that he believes to have observed: IPHEGENIA.
Cowardly who then will dive as in her, like
The organophote absolutely deployed that perpetuates
Against her the handling of a rod in the
Twist of her vagina Or better encircled bard becoming
Believable! I shift sufficiently towards
The immense tree on their left, I take a
Photo, regretting that I did not know more about
The color of the events. Jacob cowardly
Did not see a drop, despite that the other was always
Powerfully engaged in his mating.
Poor Iphigenia, to whom everyone offers their hand at last
In order to help her get up, pull down her skirt,
Burn behind the mound of dirty earth the fake
Underpants. The elastique, putting to bed the irreal.

La pince de l'homme qui, se sentant observé,
Lèvera brusquement un coude dans la direction
De ce qu'il croit avoir observé: IPHIGÉNIE.
Pleutre qui alors plongera comme en elle, comme
L'organophote absolument déployé qui perpétue
Contre elle le maniement d'une verge dans la
Tour de son ventre Ou bien barde encerclé deve-
Nant croyant! Je me déplace suffisamment vers
L'arbre immense à leur gauche, je prends une
Photo, regrettant de ne pas en savoir plus sur
La couleur et les evénements. Jacob pleutre n'y
Voit goutte, malgré que l'autre soit toujours
Fortement engagé dans son accouplement. Pauvre
Iphigénie, à qui tous tendront la main enfin
Pour l'aider à se relever, rabattre sa jupe,
Brûler derrière la motte de terre sale la culotte
Falsifiée. L'élastique, le couchant l'irréel

"And you know, when you are below, he
sees if he did not have some hope, the other…
The heroine." I wanted you to accept that all
This was only an ugly calculation with innumerable
Possibilities in bulk. Esteem and intelligence
Having taken off from the territory of San Tome, and the
Clouds having once again enshrouded the squalid
Body of Birkin (D. H. Lawrence 325 et sq.),
I will espouse the eloquence of an amphitheatre full
Of helmets, I will squirm until she
No longer stays in place, until she is transported towards
The preserved rose, the preserve erected, the vase
"of my mournful body and the heroine lowering pavil-
ion, we sleeping together" like calves, that is
That the pink of Endymion becomes that of a calf.

"Et savez-vous, quand vous êtes là-dessous, il
voir s'il n'y avait pas quelque espoir, l'autre…
L'héroine." Je voudrais que tu acceptes que tout
Ceci n'ait été qu'un vilain calcul d'innombrables
Possibilités en vrac. L'estime et l'intelligence
Ayant décollé du territoire de San Tome, et les
Nuages ayant une fois de plus enveloppé le corps
Crasseux de Birkin (D. H. Lawrence 325 et sq.),
J'épouserai l'eloquence d'un amphithéâtre empli
De casques, je me tortillerai jusqu'à ce qu'elle
Ne tinene plus en place, qu'elle s'achemine vers
La rose conserve, la conserve érigée, la situe
"de mon corps pleure et l'héroïne baissant pavil-
lon, nous couchons" comme des veaux, c'est-à-dire
Que le rose d'Endymion devient celui d'un veau.

Writing is a compound of diverse straight and curved lines, of a regular assemblage which is formed of characters from which we make different syllables and all the words of the discourse we write.

Les Eléments d'Etienne de Blégny, Expert Juror, Writer for Verification of Contested Writing, 1961.

L'écriture est un composé de diverses lignes droites et courbes, de l'assemblage régulier desquelles se forment des caractères dont on fait les différentes syllables de tous les mots du discours qui s'écrit.

Les Eléments d'Etienne de Blégny, Expert Juré, Ecrivain pour les Vérifications des Ecritures contestées, 1961.

Now the bath tub with the roe deer above
She would have known immediately what to do
De Graaf that our walks had made a deli-
Cious scandal, had revealed the dream of foolish
Emotions, capital offense that we have not the force
The farce of loving what one must, the lesson.
Something lovable in its own manner of appealing,
As if there is no quarter and that we do not
Accept any of it, among the immutable and d p ll s
V rm ns r ngs with three or more colors, fears
Crying more pelting than actual wax bubons like
Mules (Jacqueline writes to me: "Mules == slippers
Or horses. Reply quickly please"
Besançon 29/12/66.)   and like horses
        poorly placed on the tub
Because they are totally up against the deer,
That is to say douche to douche, that she oscillates
Still,
Good player in spite of all in the flow

Maintenant le bac avec les chevreuils dessus
Elle aurait su immédiatement ce qui'il y a à faire
De Graaf que nos promenades ont fait le déli-
cieux scandale, a révélé le rêve de sentiments
Insensés, injure capitale qu'on n'a pas la force
La farce de s'aimer ce qu'il faudrait, la leçon.
Quelque chose d'aimable à sa facon d'appeler,
Comme il n'y a pas de quartier et qu'on n'en
Accepte aucun, parmi les immuables et d p ll s
V rm n s r ng s a trois (ou plus) couleurs, peurs
Pleurs plus pluie qu'exacts bubons de cire comme
Mulets (Jacqueline m'écrit: "Mules == pantoufles
Ou chevaux. Répondez vite s'il vous plâit"
Besaçon 29/12/66.)   et comme chevaux
            mal placés sur le bac
Parce qu'ils sont tout contre les chevreuils,
Pour ainsi dire douche à douche, qu'elle oscille
Encore,
Bonne joueuse malgré tout dans le courant

Aeneas was the first of us who had the idea to cut words. I asked him one day with great insistence what was the reason he advocated thus; —My son, he replied to me, we cut words for three reasons; the first is to test the finesse of our pupils when they have sought out and discovered that which presents itself with some obscurity; the second is to give to language a certain pomp and beautiful lines; the third is so as not to furnish for the little ones or for the first dolt who comes along the meaning of our secret doctrines that must remain accessible only to savants alone; and this in order that the pigs do not trample upon precious pearls, as the old proverb says. In effect if they learn according to these principles, not only would they not have any reverence for their master, nor would they give witness to him either deference or respect, but moreover, like true pigs, they would tear to pieces those who have adorned them.

VIth century.

Enée est premier parmi nous que eut l'idée de couper les mots. Je lui demandai un jour avec beaucoup d'insistance pour quelle raison il agissait ainsi; —Mon fils, me répondit-il, on coupe les mots pour trois raisons; la première est d'éprouver la finesse de nos élèves lorsqu'ils ont à rechercher et à découvrir ce qui se présente avec quelque obscurité; la seconde est de donner au langage un certain apparat et de belles lignes; la troisième est de ne point faciliter aux petits ou au premier sot venu l'intelligence de nos doctrines secrètes qui ne doivent rester accessibles qu'aux seuls savants; et cela pour que les pourceaux n'aient point à piétiner des perles précieuses, comme dit le vieux proverbe. En effet s'ils étudiaient d'après ces principes, non seulement ils n'auraient aucune révérence pour leur maître, non seulement ils ne lui témoigneraient ni déférence ni respect, mais encore, comme de vrais pourceaux, ils mettraient en pièces ceux qui les ont parés.

VIe siecle.

Eros Raving continued

Éros énergumène suivi

I use, my mistress, such words of affection and love that are perhaps too unequal to your condition, but you have thus commanded me, and I think that if ever they gave me their due, it is in this act where death removes all inequality.

                                              Honoré d'Urfé

J'use, ma maîtresse, de ces paroles d'affection et d'amour qui sont peut-être trop inégales à votre condition, mais vous me l'avez ainsi commandé, et je pense que si jamais elles ont dû m'être permises, c'est en cette action où la mort ôte toute inégalité.

                                              Honoré d'Urfé

Existence that for the achievement of a confidence
To exit the palace for a good gourmand, for,
The hymen of her breasts and the melancholy therefor
Responsible and for me to relieve analogous
Examples—Resume one's place—The novel that
I first of all serve myself embarkations temple phrases,
The sentence or the place to resume primarily of
Sufficient splendor that is necessary to regard.
                              maybe even en
                                          v
Without knowing her her breasts of white theo-   y
Logy of all witness save he
Whose race testifies, ME?
She had nothing at all in having drunk but little of it
Nothing to hold back in her transports, her zone to
Him only the seduction of a nook of the pie-
Ce, her entire "hunting" figure like a schoolgirl
While the obstructed egg percolates its own
Introduction, that on the glacier treks a king

Vie que pour l'obtention d'une confidence
Sortir du palais pour un bon gourmand, or,
L'hymen de ses seins et la mélancholie qui y
Sied et de mon côté relever d'analogues
Exemples—Reprendre la place—Le roman dont
Je me sers d'abord abordages temples phrases,
La phrase ou la place à reprendre d'abord qu-
Assez d'une splendeur qu'il faut guetter,
peut-être même env
i
Sans la connaître les seins de blanche théo- e
Logie de tout témoin hormis lui   r
La race de celui qui témoigne, MOI?
Elle n'avait tout en n'ayant que peu bu
Plus de retenue dans ses transports, son parage à
Lui seul avait la séduction d'un coin de piè-
Ce, toute la figure "chasse" comme l'écolière.
Tandis que l'oeuf entravé percute sa propre
Introduction, que sur le glacier marche un roi

There is nothing else to see
The canker in our act of extreme courte-
Sy, less costly and better Astrid or divine
Good will which quite obviously no consultation
Confers. Tepidity, when I want you so much when
Breezes in the night no longer become you
Like the luxurious solitude of lobster traps!
You want to give me the historical? Read absolutely
He even will play bastard so that we see suddenly
The track disappear because it is a
Desert. Small bother if our waters lust
After sand, if my verse loves only the present,
Not love better than when I leave you emol-
Lient like your thighs as I write them a-
Bove
"Otherwise a little spirit that stands up without
Cadaver."

Il n'y a rien d'autre à voir
La plaie dans notre acte d'extrême courtoi-
Sie, moins chères et meilleures Astrid ou bien
Bonté divine où de toute evidence nul consul ne
Convient. Tiédeurs, que je vous désire quand
De brisées dans la nuit vous ne devenez pas (ou plus?)
Qu'une solitude luxueuse comme cases à homards!
Donne-moi l'historique, veux-tu? Lire absolument
Il va même prétendre salaud qu'on voit tout de
Suite disparaître la route parce que c'est un
Désert. Piètre trouble si nos eaux s'éprennent
Du sable, si mon vers n'aime que le présent,
Ne m'aime mieux que quand je sors de toi émo-
Luement comme nos flancs si je les écris ci-
Dessus
"Sinon une petite âme qui tient debout sans
Cadavre."

A risk only clothed, I plunge my fear
Completely cloaked in musk. The rest is Mozart
Do you understand? PoeTAILOR twenty years your
Senior with boot blows I bury it in a
Tree because he has no other interest here below he
Feels the earth and he is covered outside. One
Could even sustain him in marble. In mar-
Ble (but I no longer can)… The candied pear
The stupidity to believe that a swallow just
Crashed in the chaos of my last hallucination
I feel myself in a moment very violent
    before the border of the clay plate, I
Am out of breath. The lucerne is still flanked
By Mozart in final form, perhaps, that he would be to me
Necessary—when I must seek the
Kiss of thy lips at the entrance to a room—
To have for distorted peace the inscription: Peace

Un risque seulement vêtu, mon effroi je plonge
Tout habillé dans du musc. Le reste c'est Mozart
Ce que tu comprends? PoètAILLEUR vingt ans ton
Seigneur à coups de bottes je l'enterre dans un
Arbre parce qu'il n'a aucun intérêt ici-bas il
Sent la terre et il est habillé au-dehors. On
Pourrait même s'entretuer en marbre. Dans du mar-
Bre (mais je ne le peux plus)... La poire confite
La bêtise de croire qu'une hirondelle vient de se
Casser dans le chaos de ma dernière hallucination
Je me sens dans un moment très violent
    devant la bordure d'l'assiette en terre, je
Manque de souffle. La luzerne est encore flanquée
De Mozart au point, peut-être, qu'il me serait
Nécessaire—quand je devrais rechercher le
Baiser de tes lèvres à l'entrée d'une pièce—
D'avoir pour paix tordue l'inscription: Paix.

This tempest makes cartfuls of words
The dump heap of these carts engenders tenderness
Towards that crevice where I think I feel you, even a
Tiny bit drole. So sound the alarm
And who made Some thing for what I do
Not want to name, torments and sucks the water
The plants begin to grow and virtue
Hangs like a woodcock, by his beak, through
Whatever pleases you to name
This makes a good picture   with the account
On the sill, the sink en route before me-
Eting its normal destination that is come
To crush against some lips (have to have sucked you
As is his duty. It's impersonal, as one would say)
My lips. At last if the firmness of your buttocks
Obsesses me, it is that there is no further extension
To my table of trash, that finally it is no
Longer beautiful at all.

Cet orage enfin devient des charrettes de mots
Le tombereau de ces charrettes se pousse en douceur
Vers cette crevasse où je pense te sentir, même un
Tantinet drôle. Ainsi sonne l'alarme
Et qui a fait Quelque chose pour ça que je n'
Aurai pas envie de nommer, harcèle et pèle l'eau.
Les plantes commencent à grosser et la vertu
Pend comme une bécasse, par le bec, à travers
Ce qu'il vous plaira de nommer
Ici il fait bon peindre   avec la facture
Sur le rebord, l'évier en route avant de re-
Joindre sa destination normale qui est de venir
S'écraser contre des lèvres (avoir t'avoir sucée
Comme il se doit. C'est du neutre, dirait'on)
Mes lèvres. Enfin si le ferrement de ta fesse
M'obsède, c'est qu'il n'y a plus de rallonge
A ma table d'immondices, qu'enfin il ne fait
Plus beau du tout.

"DEBRIS
 FRAGMENTS,
  HORRIBLE
   ACCIDENTS"
    NIETZSCHE

"DÉBRIS
 FRAGMENTS,
  HASARDS
   HORRIBLES"
    NIETZSCHE

Who knows if I had not even been greatly be-
yond what the imagination can grasp?

SADE

Qui sait même si je n'ai pas été beaucoup au-
dessus de ce que peut saisir l'imagination?

SADE

Would she finish by returning to her place alone
The secret unconscious volupteuse, at night
Could this be even some other state of vassalage?
To flee together and knowing nothing one about
The other. The fields are the places where one makes
Harvests. The unfamiliar altitude does not lift its
Paw in order to assure us either that the manure has
Become, this year, better than last year or
In order that green and red spread the nocturnal violet
Where we cross the chains
A problem that science has yet to resolve
You have taken some very young vine shoots of fear that
Again she does not go with the foal fastened
To this neck straight and gnarled that she grasps
With her winged arms, and to which floats the purple
Crest, banner that the blood prevents from knocking

"Sauf les amoureux commençants ou finis qui
veulent commencer par la fin il y a tant de choses
qui finissent par le commencement que le commen
-cement commence à finir par être la fin la fin en
sera que les amoureux et autres finiront par com-
mencer à recommencer par ce commencement qui
aura fini par n'être que la fin retournée ce qui
commencera par être égal à l'éternité qui n'a ni
fin ni commencement et finira par être aussi fina-
lement égal à la rotation de la terre où l'on aura
fini par ne distinguer plus où commence la fin
d'où finit le commencement ce qui est toute fin de
tout commencement égale à tout commencement
de toute fin ce qui est le commencement final
de l'infini par l'indéfini. Égale une épitaphe égale
une préface et réciproquement."

Peut-être cité en 1873?

7 Sensible Poems, without Conclusion

7 Poèmes de bon sens, sans conclusion

Turning from his sweet girl that a very distant relation-

Turning from his sweet girl that a very distant relation-
Ship develops at the arrival of 3 positions,
Exaggeratedly expansive, exaggerately cordial like a…
5 minutes of reading at any rate, thus:
"As soon as she had penetrated the secret feelings
Of Mademoiselle E. she had a companion with a good
Nature, and, with a Latin education, turned out to be a
Likable young girl, gifted in natural sci."
She was enlivened a little by hillocks, rocks, vines
As soon as I lay down on a small tease of c…
And this is not today, like them, like a
Savage spring that we stir that she shrieks
And was so much the object of my care that for us to see
Knees bent she would be seized by shame and doubt,
We did not surrender naked, one on one, to common sense.

Se détournant de sa douce fille qu'un rapport très loin-

Se détournant de sa douce fille qu'un rapport très loin-
Tain développe à l'arrivée des 3ᵉ positions,
Exagérément expansif, exagérément cordial comme un…
5 minutes de lecture de toute manière, ainsi:
"Aussitôt qu'elle eut pénétré les secrets sentiments
De Mademoiselle E. elle eut une compagne d'un bon
Naturel, et, d'un roman d'éducation, sortit une
Aimable jeune fille, douée pour les sciences nat."
Elle s'anime un peu en coteaux, en rochers, en vignes
Aussitôt que je repose sur un petit taquin de c…
Et ce n'est pas aujourd'hui, comme eux, comme une
Source sauvage que nous frémissons qu'elle hurle
Et fut si bien l'objet de mes soins qu'à nous voir
Genoux ployés elle serait prise de honte et de doute
On ne se livre pas nus, à deux, au bon sens.

Our real crime is that our characters will be

Our real crime is that our characters will be
Always in quest of bumble bee hives, of
Diaper changing tables above our dear heads with the-
Me important. A landscape that destroys a part of the city
And in the final stage I would be only a regular element,
Fortuitous? Let's go then.
                              In a circumstance of the same
Date, in the sour grains in a row, in
The blackness of blood pudding with a precursor head of
Army, a same depopulation, a same Jobarderie of a
Homebody.
All that happened to him for her is natural, the thought
Of our outbreak (she in a corset and I wearing my
Silk pantaloons) in this abode of the songstress with
Her son, the idea of our love-making without putting out
The lamps, even our classic bodies.

Notre crime réel est que nos personages seront

Notre crime réel est que nos personages seront
Toujours à la recherche de nids à bourdons, de
Tables à langer au-dessus de nos chères têtes d'un thè-
Me important.Un paysage qui détruit une partie de la ville
Et au stade final je ne serais qu'un élément regulier,
Fortuit? Allons donc.
                        Dans une circonstance de même
Date, dans le grains suris d'une écossaise, dans
L'épaisseur de boudin d'une tête d'avant-coureur d'
Armée, un même dépeuplement, une même jobardise de
Casanier.
Tout ce qui se passé pour elle est naturel, la pensée
De notre irruption (elle en corset et moi portent mon
Pantalon de soie) dans cette demeure de chanteuse avec
Son fils, l'idée de notre accouplement sans éteindre
Les lampes, même nos formes classiques.

To G. for whom the hills part and lack

To G. for whom the hills part and lack
Money to develop here a game or two of columns
She and I come together for the parallel walk
That must lead us towards a lasting love. With diffi-
Culty, I do not think of ever having intended to give
An indication on her dresses or the multitudes of hooks
That ornamented the shelves of her room.
Her sensitivity (from magazines) prevents her from seeing
A boss to cut out and my presence as barman (false)
From cohabitating in the same part of her room, or better
Still the privilege of an invitation by mouth to the couch
(like "the shepherdess with musical instruments")
G. long and unbeknown in my Tub-Shower.

A G. d'où partent les collines et manquent d'

A G. d'où partent les collines et manquent d'
Argent pour y déveloper un jeu ou deux de colonnes
Elle et moi nous groupons pour la démarche parallèle
Qui doit nous mener vers un amour durable. Avec diffi-
Culté, je ne pense pas l'avoir jamais entendue donner
Une indication sur ses robes ou la multitude d'agrafes
Qui ornaient les étagères de sa chambre.
Sa délicatesse (de magazine) lui interdit de voir
Un patron à découper et ma présence de barman (faux)
Cohabiter sur une même terre de chambre, ou bien
Encore l'apanage d'une bouche d'invitée au sofa
(comme: "la bergère aux instruments de musique")
G. la longue et l'inusuelle dans mon Bains-Douches.

The position of our hearts like farms

The position of our hearts like farms
As we have already said about our transactions,
In spite of her, who is the girl and who is the sister of
Enemies when we come to a standstill there, seized by
Repulsion before some symbol of sex or of rejection?
A water flower, as she carried herself, open to the
Two Warloo blondes, without lifted eyebrows and talking
About a trick that helps them when the escapade makes
Them feel like everyone else, and this red color that par
Excellence misleads us about intentions
Stretched out on the chaise lounge, those who are around
Her lose their sweetness. Negating time. And (again
Thanking everyone), I decline the humor of it.

La mis en place de nos coeurs comme des fermes

La mis en place de nos coeurs comme des fermes
Comme nous l'avons déjà dit pour nos transactions,
Malgré lui, qui est la fille et qui est la soeur des
Ennemis quand on s'immobilise là, envahis par la
Répulsion devant quelque symbole de sexe ou de refus?
A fleur d'eau, comme elle se comportait, ouverte aux
Deux blondes de Warloo, sans sourciller et parlant d'
Une formule qui les aide quand l'équipée se fait sentir
Comme tout le monde, et cette couleur rouge qui par
Excellence nous trompe sur les intentions.
Allongée dans la chaise longue, ceux qui sont autour
D'elle perdent leur douceur. Niant l'heure. Et (j'en
Remercie le public), j'en décline l'humeur.

Poe:

"It has now become necessary that I give the facts, at least as I comprehend them myself. Succinctly here they are:"

Poe:

"Il est maintenant devenu necessaire que je donne les faits, autant du moins que je les comprends moi-même. Succinctement les voici:"

In terms of her dust which is to acquiesce with

In terms of her dust which is to acquiesce with
Prudence, the retreat of affection is a poppy.
To him who replaces her in mystic forests and who sniffs
Out well the error since one must indeed finish with the
Episode of love potion, with this duration or with the
Attention we are going to accord him is going to succeed
Like a grinding of millstone painted in the memory
Beyond the inlet of the arms of the sea, I am now
The only art within reach of her dripping arms
At gatherings she declares: "One does not cure my
Torment with a kiss, I am destroyed by a designated
Love, no longer feeling either my knees or the
Backs of my thighs."

Aux termes de sa poussière qui est d'acquiescer avec

Aux termes de sa poussière qui est d'acquiescer avec
Prudence, le retrait de l'affection est un pivot.
Lui qui la remplace en forêts mystiques et qui sent
Bien l'erreur puisqu'il en faut bien finir avec l'
Episode du philtre d'amour; à cette durée ou à l'
Attention que nous allons lui accorder va succéder
Comme un bruit de meulière peinte dans le souvenir
Par-delà l'anse du bras de mer, je suis à présent
Le seul art à la portée de ses bras ruisselants
Aux réunions elle déclare: "On ne guérit pas mon
Tourment d'un baiser, je me détruis dans un amour
Désigné, n'en sentant plus ni les genous ni les
Arrières de cuisse."

        Having once envisaged giving a
sequel
to THE HUNT AND DEPARTURE OF LOVE
in using in all and for all only poems

a collage uninterrupted by colophons moreover

cups and balls, chimney pieces, cracks, gold,

flowers printed in the leather rendering the walls.

But it requires letters very, very rich
and colophons are always the entries or the
exits of books (or D'Assoucy or Brontë, what!)
    Saint-Gelais praising *Illyrine* — year VII svp! —
But the latter participated in another collection that
will doubtless be of great value and perhaps my
VISIT OF HONOR

    thus as I demonstrate above — regarding
a poem — it came upon me to use extracts of
letters. A collection of letters (without drawings obviously) could thus follow a collection of poems,
each page of one collection recalling a precise page
of the other. But this does not explain that, beware then!

    Ayant une fois envisagé de donner une
suite
à LA CHASSE ET LE DEPART D'AMOUR
en n'utilisant en tout et pour tout de poèmes

qu'un collage ininterrompu des colophons d'alors

bilboquets, manteaux de cheminées, fêlures, ors,

fleurs imprimées dans les cuirs rendant les murs.

Mais il faudrait des lettres très, très grasses
et les colophons sont toujours des entrées ou des
sorties de livres (ou D'Assoucy ou Brontë, quoi!)
    Saint-Gelais prônant *Illyrine* — d'an VII svp! —
mais celle-ci fait partie d'un autre recueil qui
sera sans doute de grand luxe et peut-être mon
SEJOUR D'HONNEUR

    ainsi comme je le démontre ci-dessus — en regard
d'un poème — il m'arrive d'utiliser des extraits de
lettres. Un recueil de lettres (sans les dessins évidemment) pourrait ainsi suivre un recueil de poèmes,
chaque page d'un recueil renvoyant à une page précise
de l'autre. Mais ceci n'explique pas cela, gare donc!

What profundity might we make of our wounds?

What profundity might we make of our wounds?
A woman, a wounded woman, wounded by me, but
The usage of this phrase has been as if dominated
By feelings of artifices and of grandeurs (with s's)
How does SSSSSatan bring the gates on his back?
What profundity? And this presence for the last
Distant woman, clinging to me in order to avoid the
Tempest ruining her naked body of Mademoiselle BO-Y.
The meaning of the Moped at her place, heading straight
For me, after having jumped over both porches
Of marriage. (Puritan dove, a century la-
Ter)… Belated sexual pleasure equals public outcry.

De quelle profondeur ne s'y ferait-on des plaies?

De quelle profondeur ne s'y ferait-on des plaies?
Une femme, a wounded woman, blessée par moi, Mais
L'usage dans cette phrase a été comme d'être dominés
Par des sentiments d'astuces et de noblesses (avec des s)
Comment SSSSSatan amenait-il des portes sur son dos?
Quelle profondeur? Et cette présence pour la dernière
Femme loin, serrée contre moi pour éviter que la
Tempête n'abîme son corps nu de Mademoiselle BO-Y.
Le sens de la bécane chez lui, en venant droit
Sur moi, après avoir franchi tous deux le porche
Des marriages. (Puritaine colombe, un siècle plus
Tard)… Volupté tardive égale clameurs publiques.

At her entrance she is going to tell me that she

At her entrance she is going to tell me that she
To tell me the state of horror, ravishing but that she
Hidden, by contrast her human suffocation
"We put the knife to the throat," he
Takes her back with the knowledge of butting her, of
Hitting her against the wood, of licking her, calmed
Because garglings can calm the
Bad letters, brazen beard and finally some
Other news. Miscounted hearts that you survive
By your little finger…" In your widowhood which a
Moral history intervenes, that at last in
Time, having created a bureau of pu-
Blic relations, she was going to throw herself into a coma.

Dès son entrée elle va me répondre qu'elle

Dès son entrée elle va me répondre qu'elle
Me dire l'état d'horreur, ravissante mais qu'elle
Dérobée; par contre son étouffement humain
"Nous mettez le couteau sur la gorge", il
La reprend avec la conscience de la butter, de la
Cogner contre le bois, de la lécher, calmée
Parce que les gargarismes peuvent calmer les
Lettres mauvaises, barbe éhontée et enfin d'
Autres nouvelles. Coeurs de mécomptes qui survivez
Dès son petit doigt…" Dans son veuvage qu'une
Histoire morale intervenue, qu'enfin à
Temps, ayant créé un bureau de relations pu-
Bliques, elle allait se lancer dans le coma.

Poem of 29 April 1962

Poème du 29 avril 1962

Poetry transforms everything into words
and into verbal signs.

NOVALIS

La poésie transforme tout en mots
et en signes verbaux

NOVALIS

1.

A. by Capdenac and Villefranche-de-Rouergue
B. by Capdenac and Rodez 36
    from Albi to Toulouse
S.N.C.F. == National Society of French
                        Railroads
"there is always a noble Genovese on the way to beg
pardon of some sovereign of stupidities that their
Republic makes" (*Voyage de Gratz à La Haye*, by Montesquieu, the latter having left Genoa 20/11/1728)
He had already said above on page 628: "that he
collected in the marquisate 36,000 barrels of oil,
which I can hardly believe." (end of citation)

… generals Marbot, Lamoricière, Espinasse, Caffarelli,
Bentzmann, Laperrine
…the room of Father Lacordaire with his furnishings
…superb park extends to the foot of the black
Mountain, bordered by a beautiful path and enclosed by
Magnificent green masses, following the forest path that
Continues to climb up the valley.
These are gorgeous promenades (summer camps
Of the P. and T.) giving a series of letters before 2 Oct.

1.

A. par Capdenac et Villefranche-de-Rouergue
B. par Capdenac et Rodez 36
    d'Albi à Toulouse
    S.N.C.F. == Société Nationale des Chemins de Fer
Français
   "il ya toujours un noble gênois en chemin pour deman-
   der pardon à quelque souverain des sottises que leur
   République fait" (*Voyage de Gratz à La Haye*, de Mon-
   tesquieu, celui-ci étant parti de Gênes le 20/11/1728)
   Il avait déjà dit en haut de la page 628: "qu'il se
   cueillait dans le marquisat 36 000 barils d'huile;
   ce que j'ai peine à croire." (fin de la citation.)

   …généraux Marbot, Lamoricière, Espinasse, Caffarelli,
   Bentzmann, Laperrine
   …la chambre du père Lacordaire avec son mobilier
   …superbe parc s'étendant jusqu'au pied de la montagne
   Noire, bordé d'une belle allée et entouré de magnifiques
   Masses de verdure, en suivant la route forestière qui
   Continue de remonter le vallon.
   Ce sont de ravissante promenades (colonie de vacances
   Des P. et T.) donner suite aux lettres avant le 2 Oct.

Le ROBINET (page 558, 50ᵉ §)
    A series of charming cascades near my living quarters at the base of an arch 75 m long not any large fountain of water without special authorization of the chief engineer who resides at Allauch
(by telephoning at 63 one can have prepared a good meal)

And now the problem of the D.I.F. (*District International Farm*):
Not because they dispense but the place is
not so badly situated as that (it is on a nipple),
One sees

2.

Nearly all along the coast
There was not a site of attraction more majestic
The mountains covered with small houses created
A very beautiful effect, but the station declined and disappeared
In those of Kleiner Hafner and of Männedorf (lake of Zurich) in one of those of Mount See (Haute-Austria), for not having undergone a violent fire

Le ROBINET (page 558, 50ᵉ §)
>Une suite de charmantes cascades auprès des mé-
nages   au fond d'une voûte de 75 m de long
pas de grand jet d'eau sans un autorisation
spéciale de l'ingénieur en chef qui réside à
Allauch
(en téléphonant au 63 on se fait faire un bon repas)

Et maintenant le problème du D.I.F. (*District Inter-
national Farm*):
Non pas parce qu'ils dépensent mais le lieu n'étant
pas si mal situé que ça (il est sur un mamelon),
On voit

2.

Presque tout le long de la côte
Il n'était pas de lieu d'attirance plus majestueux
Les montagnes couvertes de petites maisons faisaient
Un très bel effet, mais la station déclina et dispa-
rut
Dans celles de Kleiner Hafner et de Männedorf (lac
de Zurich) dans une de celles du mont See (Haute-
Autriche), pour ne pas avoir à subir un feu violent

But it strikes the eye that they do not contribute
Practically to any of these destinations.

Broken line for the pattern EFGHJKLMO

Summit E
Summit F   etc.
Summit G   etc.
Summit H   etc.
Summit J   etc.
K in contact with the rail
LMO contour to determine the natural reservoir

Circular of the intendants on the shards remaining
In the confines of the royal hospitals: Soissons
Being effectively one of the most beautiful ensembles
One recalls the tasteful gathering of literature here
Medical as well as *educational* treating the
Case Léger who ate "without cooking it"
The heart of a young girl;
The case Papavoine who engorged two beautiful children
Although he did not know them from Eve or Adam
The case of Henriette Cornier who cut off the head of an
Infant

Mais il saute aux yeux qu'ils ne se prêtent
Pratiquement à aucune de ces destinations.

Ligne brisée pour le gabarit EFGHJKLMO

Sommet E
Sommet F   etc.
Sommet G   etc.
Sommet H   etc.
Sommet J   etc.
K au contact du rail
LMO contour à déterminer du réservoir naturel

Circulaire des intendants sur les obus subsistant
Dans l'enceinte des hopitaux royaux: Soissons
Etant effectivement l'un des plus beaux ensembles
On crut de bon ton d'y rassembler la littérature
Aussi bien médicale que d'*éducation* traitant du
Cas Léger qui avait mangé "sans le faire cuire"
Un coeur de jeune fille;
Le cas Papavoine qui égorgea deux beaux enfants
Alors qu'il ne les connaissait ni d'Eve ni d'Adam
Le cas d'Henriette Cornier qui coupa la tête d'un
Enfant

In England the Bowler affair
In Germany the Siever affair…
"if we were standing together on a rock"

Bridge on the road of the fruit farmers
Bridge Saint-Maxence
Bridge of Basses-Granges (Orléans to Tours) Bridge from Couturettes to Arbois, Bridge of Paisia that is in a handle of a basket. Relative to the blazing of pieces compressed.

3.

La Ferté-Macé (Aude) at the peak of the lilacs
"chance is not a train that passes every day
at the same time. It is a prostitute who offers herself fugitively, then goes on to the arms of another". (Notebooks of Count Ciano.)
for murders that were committed on the railway
102 see Rachele Peyrats IX, 28-220…
In small villages like Pèzenas, Uzès, Viviers

For, when we are well, we may feel very easily
this disgust, and, better still, we have encountered the most helpful concourse of the forest landscape (at the moment of the

En Angleterre l'affaire Bowler
En Allemagne l'affaire Sievert...
"si nous étions debout tous deux sur un rocher"

Pont sur le chemin des fruitiers
Pont Saint-Maxence
Pont des Basses-Granges (Orléans à Tours) Pont de
Couturettes à Arbois, Pont de Paisia qui est en anse
de panier. Relatives au flamboiement des pièces com-
primées.

3.

La Ferté-Macé (Aude) au sommet des lilas
"la chance n'est pas un train qui passé chaque jour
à la même heure. C'est une prostituée qui s'offre fu-
gitivement, puis passe au bras d'un autre". (Carnets
du comte Ciano.)
pour ce qui était des meurtres commis sur la voie ferrée
102 voir Rachele Peyrats IX, 28-220...
Des petites bourgades comme Pèzenas, Uzès, Viviers

Or, quand nous sommes bien, on peut sentir très facilement
ce dégout, et, bien mieux, nous avons rencontré le concours
le plus obligeant du paysage forestier (au moment de la

greatest spiciness of the chestnut trees), these able
to spread over kms, at sharp angles to the road,
in the domain of Ayérac.

After some time the bombardment begins again,
A leaden sun and at a short distance from the Basque
Positions, at the frontiers of those whom we looked upon
As frothing with their domestic animals and
Their livestock which did not prevent them coming in the
Evening or during siesta in the afternoon to exchange
Pieces of tile or some combat photographs

Many cry and leave without money, their
Debts abandoned to the leniency that is
Clemency without course and thirst of
Autumn
I give thanks again:
    —The *aerial Raids* as well as the guards of the
barrage Jessup who was then in committee;
    —Hélène B. who was to me precious;
    —Heaven that allowed me to follow just as
close the *Steering Committees for Hunger*

plus grande verdeur des châtaigniers), celui-ci pouvant
s'étendre sur des kms, aux angles brusques de la route,
au domaine d'Ayérac.

Après un certain temps le bombardement recommençait,
Un soleil de plomb et à faible distance des positions
Basques, aux frontiers de ceux que l'on regardait
Comme les *écumants* avec leurs animaux domestiques et
Leur bétail ce qui ne les empêchait pas le soir venu
Ou pendant la sieste de l'après-midi d'échanger des
Pieces de toitures ou quelque photographie de combat

Beaucoup pleurent et partent sans argent, leurs
Arrières s'abandonnent à la mansuétude qui est
La douceur sans chemins et la soif de l'arrière-
Saison
Je remercie:
    —Les *Raids aériens* ainsi que les gardiens du
barrage Jessup qui étaient alors en comité;
    —Hélène B. qui m'a été précieuse;
    —Le ciel de m'avoir permis de suivre d'aussi
près le *Comités volants pour la Faim*

4.

Saint-Denis près Martel (buffet facing directly
on the quay, but it closes at midnight)
With his violence and his anger: one is self-styled
Inclined to flee them to avoid this spectacle in the course
Of which a legitimate terror wins and makes you flee
Finally.
"station of sorrow and of regeneration"
A little further on, Junney had installed de-
pots: their range will cover more than 600 ha where
Yet passes for fifteen days an Alsatian mill-
stone.
    Appleton by C°
C.c. Journey Junior will take count of your proofs, for
He restricts everything of your passage (or respects?)
Have confidence in C.c. Journey Junior throughout the year!
Question (?):
    WHAT NOVELS HAVE YOU WRITTEN?
"however on his face which he saw from afar"… he
Pursued for a few moments his reverie before
Returning again to write before his wide open window
Feeling himself at his wit's end perhaps because of
The heat.

4.

Saint-Denis près Martel (buffet donnant directement
sur le quai, mais il ferme à minuit)
A ses violences et à ses fureurs: on est soi-disant
Porté à les fuir pour éviter ce spectacle au cours
Duquel une légitime épouvante vous gagne et fait fuir
Enfin.
"station de la douleur et de la régénérescence"
Un peu plus loin, Junney doit faire installer les en-
trepôts; leur éventail couvrira plus de 600 ha où
Passent encore pendant quinze jours une meule alsaci-
enne.
    Appleton by C°
C.c. Journey Junior tiendra compte de vos gages, car
Il restreint tout sur son passage (ou respecte?)
Ayez confiance en C.c. Journey Junior tte l'année!
Question (?):
    QUELS ROMANS ECRIVEZ-VOUS?
"cependant sur son visage qu'il voyait au loin"… il
Poursuivait quelques instants sa rêverie avant de se
Remettre à écrire devant sa fenêtre largement ouverte
En se sentant à toute extrémité peut-être à cause de
La chaleur.

Julie: "I think that these are the children who
are returning, I will take them to you at the libra-
ry in a quarter of an hour, do you want?... "Here
Occurs a crossed-out fragment in the manuscript of
Julie   To review later

3/ the history of the dislocated body of this aviator was
   very unlikely. It could not be found exact-
   ly *under that apple tree there*, is that not so?
4/ Hernandez 118

Reviewing the habits of Julie in the file on
The chair, within reach of the bathtub *savor*
desolating of linen == "colossal representation—
colossal space", one must write lips under
thy pat, Julie, that they are of a beauty clear-
ly foreseen
            stiff house hidden by a thick
curtain of trees from the eyes of strollers habi-
tuées of the cove
because she is not so distant from the ensemble
Industrial dependent on *Q Valley*, no?

Julie: "je pense que ce sont les enfants qui rentrent, je vous les amènerai à la bibliotheque dans un quart d'heure, voulez-vous?... "Ici Se place un fragment biffé sur le manuscrit de Julie   A revoir plus tard

3/ l'histoire du corps disloqué de cet aviateur était peu vraisemblable. Il ne pouvait se trouver exactement *sous ce pommier-là*, n'est-ce pas?
4/ hernandez 118.

Revoyant les habits de Julie sur le dossier de La chaise, à portée de la baignoire *goût* désolant du linge == "représentation colossale— espace colossal", il faut écrire des lèvres sous ta motte, Julie, qu'elles sont d'une beauté clairement prévue
          maison roide cachée par un épais rideau d'arbres aux yeux des promeneuses habituées de la crique
parce qu'elle n'est pas si distante de l'ensemble Industriel dépendant de *Q Valley*, non?

5.

Rustling of water she calls me from the balcony

Ah you see who now lives with the count, near
The canal, who fishes high up from his window?...
This ruined region where I descend into the forest
In order to ford the river in a reverse direction, guiding
Myself by the rays of the sun
I preserve a fond memory of this little structure and
Its round towers
On the terrace a monument to the rogue poet François
Fabie (1846-1928) by Mark Robert (1933)

Still some escarpments and here we are

Social History of Extracting. Ch. Plimer-Mordayle.
A Page from the History of Culture, unedited.
1933 *Custom Magazine.*

5.

Ruisselante d'eau elle m'appelle du balcon

Ah voyez qui maintenant demeure chez le comte, près
Du canal, qui repêche du haut de sa fenêtre?...
Cette région accidentée où je descends dans la forêt
Pour franchir la rivière en sens inverse, me guidant
Aux rayons du soleil
Je conserve un bon souvenir de cette bâtisse et de
Ses tours rondes
Sur la terrasse un monument au poète rouergat François
Fabie (1846-1928) par Mark Robert (1933)

Encore quelques escarpements et nous y sommes.

Social History of Extracting. Ch. Plimer-Mordayle.
Une page de l'histoire de la culture, inédit.
1933 *Custom Magazine.*

Biography and Bibliography of Denis Roche

Biographical Highlights

Denis Roche was born in Paris in 1937. From 1964 to 1970, he was Literary Director at Éditions Tchou. From 1962 to 1972, he participated as a member of the Director's Committee for the review Tel Quel, and under this imprint he published his first four books. In 1971, he joined Éditions du Seuil. As a member of the Editorial Committee, he directed, notably, the collections of contemporary literature, "Fiction & Cie" and "The Contemporaries." In 1980, he founded, with Gilles Mora, Bernard Plossu and Claude Nori, Cahiers de la photographie (Photographic Notebooks). He is a member of the jury of the Prix Medici. In 1997, he received the Grand Prize for Photography from the City of Paris. Denis Roche has published some twenty books since *Récits complets* in 1963. His book, *Le Boîtier de mélancolie*, published by Hazan in 1999, received the Prix André Malraux.

He began to exhibit and publish his photographs in 1978, with *Notre antéfixe*, which was the first publication of what became known afterwards as "photoautobiography." But it was especially with *La Disparition des lucioles*, in 1982, a collection of texts on the photographic act, that he attracted the attention of international critics. Numerous exhibitions then followed: in France at the Gallery Maeght, at l'Espace photographique de Paris, and at the gallery Le Réverbère at Lyon; at Brussels, Hanover, Frankfurt, Turin, Naples, Atlanta, and New York; but also in Mexico, Austria, Peru, Egypt, Japan, and Syria, among others. A critical monograph of his photographic oeuvre, gathering together texts from a dozen authors, was published in 1989 under the title *Denis Roche* (Cahiers de la photographie, No. 23).

In 1991, at Éditions Maeght, he published an album titled *Ellipse et laps* that brought together the essential work of his photographic oeuvre of this period. Then, in March 2001, Gilles Mora dedicated to Roche an important chronological monograph titled *Denis Roche - Les Preuves du temps,* a co-edition of Éditions du Seuil and Maison européenne de la photography (European House of Photography). This important monograph retraces all of Roche's work from 1971. The publication of this monograph in 2001 coincided with a general retrospective of Roche's photographs at musée Nicéphore Niepce, at Chalon-sur-Saône, and with a more experimental exhibition of his photographs at Galerie Le Réverbère, at Lyon, titled La *Question que je pose* (The *Question that I pose)*. Both exhibitions were then shown together at Paris at la Maison européenne de la photographie.

Selected Solo Exhibitions

1978 Galerie L'oeil 2000, Chateauroux

1979 Canon Photo Galerie, Geneva, Switzerland

1980 Galerie Déclinaisons, Rouen
Centre Culturel franco-italien, Turin, Italy

1981 Institut supérieur pour l'étude du langage plastique (ISELP), Brussels

1985 *Menées photographiques,* Galerie J. et J. Donguy, Paris

1986 Galerie Images Nouvelles, Bordeaux
Musée d'Art moderne, Vienna, Austria
Fulton County Public Library, Atlanta, Georgia, USA

1987 Frankfurter Kunstverein, Frankfort, Germany
Musée de Tijuana, Tiajuana, Mexico
Musée d'Art Moderne de Mexico

1988 *L'Art des circonstances,* Centre culturel français, Cairo, Egypt

1989 Le Mas de l'enfant, Barbentane (RIP, Arles)
Espace photographique de Paris, Paris
Galerie Le Réverbère, Lyon

1990 Artothèque Grand'Place, Grenoble

1991 Galerie Maeght, Paris
Alliance française, Lima, Péru

1992 Galerie municipale du Château d'Eau, Toulouse

1994 Artothèque, Vitré
Centre régional de la photographie Nord-Pas-de-Calais, Douchy-les Mines
1995 Galerie Zeit-Foto Salon, Tokyo, Japan

1996 *Il n'y a pas de leçon des Ténèbres,* Galerie Le Réverbère, Lyon
Il n'y a pas de leçon des Ténèbres, Saint-Gervais, Geneva, Switzerland
Il n'y a pas de leçon des Ténèbres, Galerie J. et J. Donguy, Paris

1997 Encontros da Imagem, Braga, Portugal
Galerie Archi typographies, Bordeaux

1998 Université Saint-Esprit de Kaslik, Beyrouth, Lebanon

1999 *Florence ilenri - Denis Roche,* Rencontres Internationales de la Photographie, Arles

2000 Centre culturel français, Damas, Syria
Hôpitaux universitaires Belle-Idée, Geneva, Switzerland

2001 La *question que je pose,* Galerie Le Réverbère, Lyon
Les preuves du temps, Musée Nicéphore Niepee, Chalon sur Saône
Les preuves du temps, Maison européenne de la photographie, Paris

Selected Group Exhibitions

1981 *Autoportraits photographiques,* Centre Georges Pompidou, Paris

1982 *Art et Littérature,* Musée d'Art moderne de la Ville de Paris

1984 *Nouvelles tendances de la recherche dans la photographie européenne,* Centro Studi Posilippo, Naples, Italy

Photographie contemporaine en France, Centre Georges Pompidou, Paris

1985 *L'Acte du photographe,* Tour Palmer, Cenon, Bordeaux

1987 *Jeune photographie,* Galerie municipale du Château d'Eau, Toulouse

1988 *Art or Nature,* barbican Art Gallery, London, England
Etat de siège, Ecole nationale supérieure des Beaux-Arts, Paris
Splendeurs et misères du corps, Musée d'Art et d'Histoire, Fribourg,
Switzerland, then at the Musée d'Art Moderne de la Ville de Paris
Fotovision -Projekt Fotografie nach 150 jahren, Sprengel Museum, Hanovre, R.F.A.

1989 *20 ans de photographie créative en France,* Leverkusen, Germany

1990 *A Fotographia actual em França,* Fondation Guibenkian, Lisbon, Portugal

1991 *Photographie actuelle en France,* Institute for Contempory Photography, New York, USA

Galerie Maeght, Paris
Alliance française, Lima, Péru

1992 La *Photographie française en liberté,* Kawasaki Museum, Tokyo then Lisbon, New York, Mexico, New Orléans
Galerie municipale du Château d'Eau, Toulouse

1994 Artothèque, Vitré
Centre régional de la photographie Nord-Pas-de-Calais, Douchy-les-Mines

1995 Galerie Zeit-Foto Salon, Tokyo, Japan
Il n'y a pas de leçon des Ténèbres, Galerie Le Réverbère, Lyon

1996 *Il n'y a pas de leçon des Ténèbres,* Saint-Gervais, Geneva, Switzerland
Il n'y a pas de leçon des Ténèbres, Galerie J. et J. Donguy, Paris

1997 Encontros da Imagem, Braga, Portugal
Galerie Archi typographies, Bordeaux

1998 Université Saint-Esprit de Kaslik, Beyrouth, Lebanon

1999 *Florence Henri - Denis Roche,* Rencontres Internationales de la Photographie, Arles

2000 Centre culturel français, Damas, Syria
Hopitaux universitaires Belle-Idée, Geneva, Switzerland

2001 La *question que je pose,* Galerie Le Réverbère, Lyon
Les preuves du temps, Musée Nicéphore Niepce, Chalon sur Saône
Les preuves du temps, Maison européenne de la photographie, Paris

Books by Denis Roche

With Éditions du Seuil:
Forestière Amazonide, Écrire 11, 1962

Récits complets, collection Tel Quel, 1963

Les Idées centésimales de Miss Elanize, collection Tel Quel, 1964

Eros énergumène, collection Tel Quel, 1968

Le Mécrit, collection Tel Quel, 1972

Louve basse, collection Tel Quel, 1972

Dépôts de savoir & de technique, collection Fiction & Cie, 1980

L'Hexaméron (en collaboration), collection Fiction & Cie, 1990

Dans la Maison du Sphinx, collection La Librairie du XXËme siècle, 1992

La Poésie est inadmissible, collection Fiction & Cie, 1995

With other publishers:
Carnac, ou les mésaventures de la narration, Tchou 1969 ; Pauvert 1985

3 Pourrissements poétiques, l'Herne, 1972

Notre antéfixe, Flammarion, 1978

Antéfixe de Françoise Peyrot, Orange Export, 1978

A quoi sert le lynx? A rien, comme Mozart, Muro Torto, 1980

Légendes de Denis Roche, Gris banal éditeur, 1981

La disparition des lucioles, L'Etoile, 1982

Conversations avec le temps, Le Castor astral, 1985

A Varèse, William Blake & Cie, 1986

Ecrits momentanés chroniques photo du magazine City 1984-87, Paris Audiovisuel, 1988

Photolalies, Argraphie, 1988

Prose au devant d'une femme, Fourbis, 1988

Ellipse et laps, Maeght, 1991

Lettre ouverte à quelques amis et à un certain nombre de jean-foutres, Fourbis, 1988

L'embarquement pour Mercure (avec Michel Butor), Le Point du Jour, 1996

Le Boîtier de mélancolie, La Photographie en 100 photographies, Hazan, 1999

Notes on Poems and Translation

Pages 24–25: This is a difficult little poem to translate because it is full of oblique and hidden references. The "blés" wheat, grains, seeds, money? all appear in other poems. This erotic little poem obviously describes again their sex act, coitus and intercourse, and love play. There is some progress here in their lovemaking revealed by maturity (or "écheance" could mean "term, expiration date"). "Sans raie" means without a part, like hair that has a part, or parts, to separate out the different groupings or layering. And then of course he mentions immediately her black hair.

Pages 26–27: Line 1: "s'installer" has the sense of "settle in, "move in." I think it is better to retain the idea of "install yourself," which also retains the line break and double entendre meant by Roche, and uses "Install" which keeps exactly the visual look in French.

Line 3: The meaning of "quitte" is also "to be even, "pay back," "be rid of," etc., but it is difficult to retain the multiple meanings intended. Is the sense of "trés vive de nu," very quickly laid bare," which would serve well and also keep the multiple meanings of naked sensuality and something revealed.

Pages 28–29: Line 2: I did the best I could with "l'éclaboussant gésier des gentianes." There's probably some hidden meaning to "gizzard," which I almost translated as "geezer" as in "old geezer," which might actually be better as a translation to keep closer to the sense of the original. I wish I had been able to find a just translation for "cor-/Dons" that retains the double entendre of cord/"heart"/core and "Dons" (gifts) and the English "dons." I finally went with "hand-/Cuffs" because it has a nice double meaning at the line break with the two meanings going back and forth as with "cor-/Dons" and in addition the image of handcuffs has latent sexuality, bondage, sado-masochism and sexual prisoner, which I believe these poems are partly about: The Enslavement of Love.

Line 6: I did the best I could also with "Chemise de nuit sur les revues couleurs, et"... I went with "folies" like the Folies Bergères for the translation of "revues couleurs."

Line 17: Another meaning of "coup" in the last line is "fuck," but it was very difficult to retain the meaning of being struck, surprised, and also the sexual meaning. I thought at least "blow" has the other meaning in English of "blow job."

Pages 30–31: Line 2: "Été," I think Roche does intend both "summer" and "been"/"was" very difficult to duplicate in English; that is, to find a word in English that means both things as in French. After I wrote "SummerWas" I liked it that way.

Line 9: "Troc," I assume refers to the Trocadero theater (ball) and of course "troc" also means to "swap," so I combined the idea of love-swapping and ravishing the way I have done.

Pages 48–49: Difficult to translate precisely lines 4-6: The paraphrasis is so convoluted and "polite" that the underlying sexual meaning is literally obscured by the literal. I think the meaning here is really something like: "What poetry it is at last to bury your prick in the earthy hole of a woman (jupes=woman, chick, broad, babe) who like the mouth of a clay jar is made to be corked or plugged." I took the "dirty" route for "les jupes" and opted for "slits." In English to state, literally, that "poetry finally forced into a clay hole does not like skirts from which one makes corks (plugs, tampons, stoppers), is total nonsense. Without reading literally the idioms and extracting the slang meaning from the surface expressions, this statement has no sense or consistency. I guess you could make a stopper out of "skirts" or out of anything for that matter, but what a mixed metaphor and poorly constructed image this would be. Skirts stuffed in a clay hole as a cork which poetry doesn't like? Where have we gotten to—visually? Especially as he starts the poem out with an image of using the edge of the tablecloth (presumably hers) to wipe off his dick wet with her pungent puntang .

And then he introduces the image of the Puritan dunkingstool, which I also take to be another allusion to his cock dipping in her pool. And why now all at once a Puritan, supposedly because he may have had a momentary change of heart and gave her something to wear to cover herself, which in fact only postpones his inevitable assault on her.

Pages 54–55: "le passement"— Larousse provides "braided" or "trimmings." And the modern meaning from football (soccer) of nutmegging a player, passing the ball between an opponent's legs. These are obviously not the meanings intended here, where the reference is to Littré and the explanation obviously describes some kind of "dip" through which leather is passed to soften, stretch, or swell it. I chose the word "dip" and "dipping" because, again the image here is of the cock increasing, stretching, swelling, "engorging," meaning maybe even in someone's throat—glottis?

Uncertain meaning of "garde tendue de Jouy." This poem is obviously a memory and poetic remembrance of a lovemaking session in Jouy. Who then is D'Estrevaillieres? Maximilien Paul Littré (1801-1881), the French lexicographer, gives the following definitions of "passement":

1. Cuve pleine d'une liqueur acide, dans laquelle le tanneur passe les peaux pour les faire gonfler. Les cuirs à l'orge sont ceux pour le travail desquels on fait aigrir de la pâte de farine d'orge.... on nomme passement, dans cette méthode, ce qui se nomme plain dans celle de la chaux, Dict. des arts et mét. Amst. 1767. Tanneur.
2. Ancien terme d'administration. Pouvoir de passer les actes publics.
3. Tissu plat de fil d'or, de soie, etc. qui sert à orner des habits, des meubles, etc. *On publie à son de trompe et cri public par les carrefours de Paris l'ordonnance du roi contre les passements d'or et d'argent, les dentelles, les points de Gêne, de Venise et de Raguse, les carrosses dorés et autres superfluités,* **GUI PATIN,** *Lettr. t. II, p. 257. Jamais on n'a vu la magnificence campagnarde si naturellement étalée, le clinquant rouillé, les passements ternis, le taffetas rayé....,* **HAMILTON,** *Gramm. XI.* Dentelle dont on bordait un habit, des manchettes, etc.
4. XIVe s. *Toute delettacion est generation, c'est à dire flus et passement de aucune chose sensible en notre nature,* **ORESME,** *Eth. 219.*
5. XVIe s. *Collets de maroquin de toutes couleurs, à passement d'or et d'argent,* **CARL., V, 32.** *Pour tondre les bordures, passemens, et autres parties estans en ligne droite [dans les jardins], convient retendre le cordeau,* **O. DE SERRES, 585,** *etc.*
6. Provenç. passamen ; espagn. pasamiento ; ital. passamento, action de passer (Voy. "PASSER"). Cette signification s'est étendue aux passements, parce qu'ils passent, s'étendent sur l'habit, sur le meuble. L'espagnol et l'italien pasamano, passamano, viennent de pasar, passar, passer, et mano, main.

There is a revealing discovery in these definitions. Here we see where Roche got his "speech," his "words." Besides the direct quote, we have here "flus" (fluxion) from Oresme; we have "en droite ligne," put directly into the poem, and "tissue plat de fil d'or, de soie," which he transforms into "piècettes du tissue ancient". We have also "la glotte passant." This shows Roche's poetic mind at work, using what he finds and transforming it to his poetic purpose.

Pages 56–57: This poem is obviously about tumescence/detumesence and sustaining the upright prick of love to prolong lovemaking, mixed with metaphors of "sustained" speech and language (words, to that effect). This is all done to music and the swoop and sweep of song or orchestration and staged drama. For want of better meaning I translated "des pots scène" as "onstage sets" but could this mean, perhaps, "footlights"? "Fournée" does mean, apparently, a fresh-baked or newly cooked batch of something. I at first had written the line fresh-baked/Funeral batch, then fresh/baked funeral batch, and then finally went with just fresh/Funeral batch."

Pages 62–63: This was one of the more difficult poems to translate because the exact words Roche uses are very specific to the subject (object) at hand but imply so much more than is at hand. This allows for great latitude in interpretation and meaning, and makes translation therefore verge. The phrase "en mêlant," for example, means precisely to "meddle with" but he also means besides "muddling and meddling with the words," "blending" together of air, words, and music. I take this to be the music of lovemaking, actual music that they may be listening to, and the "music" of the scene—bed-wave-blanket and the "Berline de merles," which in reality is a type of glass partitioned carriage. He also wants to include the quote and the idea of the glowing neck of the blacksmith horseshoer (farrier). But I think here that Roche has also in mind Wallace Steven's poem, "Thirteen Ways of Looking at a Blackbird," which includes a stanza (XI) about the shadow of the "equipage" of the carriage being mistaken by the narrator for "blackbirds"—very eerie and moving in a Poe-gothic kind of setting that stays forever in your mind: The shadow of the carriage of Death moving across the landscape with the blackbirds conspiring.

Then quite suddenly the young blond handsome young man (ephebe) comes in and the crowded (loaded) truck, a Ford or a Mack? Could this be a sexual encounter in America while hitchhiking? These poems are so full of life, emotion, and immediacy: sex and indeterminancy. These are the "pulsion" of life.

Then the "front" (brow, forehead, bumper of the vehicles?) shoving, pushing the green pasture or "range," the war, the battle of sex and nourishment. Are we talking here about the penis as a lorry pushing into the bushy landscape of the pussy and the mountain there? And what I translate as "mons" certainly could easily be just a mountain in the landscape, but then the sexual implication would be lost. And how about "Shelley's liver"? We know that Trelawny plucked his heart from the funeral pyre on the beach in Italy. Who has the liver? And the quote frames the poem like a Gothic Poetic Portrait. What a picture. Quel mélange! What kind of love encounter is this?

Littré also gives a meaning of "merle" as shading into deception and evil. This reminds me of Madame Merle in James's *Portrait of a Lady*. So in reality a "Berline de merles", could just be a "dark carriage." I think therefore that "Carriage with blackbirds" is as good as I can do. The carriage could also have blackbirds painted on it. In any case, the carriage actually "takes us" out of the interior roomscape to the exterior landscape. Fun and complex because fun and complex.

Pages 64–65: "Lie" may come from "lier" with its multiple meanings of "bond," "link," "tie," but also the word means "dregs" or "sediment" or "sludge" as in the dregs of wine, in English, "lees." Difficult to know here. "S'en est allee" I take to mean passed away, gone away, deceased, passed on, etc.

Pages 66–67: The last line of this poem of course calls up the Romance of Tristan and Iseult, where the incorrect color signal of the hoisted sail creates a tragic end for the lovers. This is the allusion here of the "drapeaux marins," which I was tempted to translate as "ship semaphores," but then "sea flags" seems more visual and immediate and keeps the image in the mind's eye of boats with flying colors. The epigrammatic quote at the beginning and end seems to me to convey the meaning that "things are only as I describe or tell them," in this case the predicated sad ending to their love affair.

Pages 68–69: Presumably the "general meaning" of this poem is a lament for their past love (fucking; I assume that the "f." stands for "foutre" and would translate the same in English as "fucking," that is why I left the "f." alone as written) and she somehow taking literally his words (verses, poems), that has somehow led to this condition of ennui, and worn out and tired story ("Édition rompu") of their fragmented and failed lovemaking, where the energy (rage, lust, "foudre"= fucking) has petered out.

The last line literally says something different than how I have translated it, but I think that the intention is as I have stated, only perhaps my rendition misses the idea of garlic (odor, potency?) as also applied to the woman, lover, her smell and pungency? I may be off base here and reading too much in, but I think this the import of this poem.

I also am not certain whether or not "combien je/Suis heureuse" shouldn't be translated "how many times I am happy," which is an odd tense mixture but might convey the idea of how many times she was satisfied, achieved orgasm.

The reference to religious paintings, panels, and implied cruxifixion (blood, feet) seems to me to indicate a holy and predicated sacrifice of the corpus of their love to the objects of quiddity, the mundane that finally comes to kill, wear out and break down all holy things. "How could you believe literally what I said?"

Page 73: Assoucy, Charles d'. (1605-1678) "L'Ovide en belle humeur." 1650. [Les métamorphoses d'Ovide en vers burlesques].

Besides his burlesque "Le Judgement de Paris," d'Assoucy's versions of the Metamorphoses include "Les Amours de Jupiter et d'Io" followed by the last poem in the work, titled "Io Furieuse," whose last verses are quoted by Roche. In the account of the amours of Jupiter and Io, Io never undresses. What does the abbreviation O B mean? Is it an abbreviation for Ovid, whose full name is Publius Ovidius Naso? The narrative following recounts the typical anger of Juno and the pleading of Jupiter to be forgiven and then the return of Io to her former state with elevation to the condition of a goddess, except of course her virginity ("fors pucelage"), which is gone forever. Roche also borrows other phrases, ideas, and language "instances" (images) from d'Assoucy's "Ovide en belle humeur" (see pp. 140-143).

Pages 74 – 75: Too bad I cannot find a way to translate "Chansons de vieille roche" to maintain the intended pun and double entendre of "Old Roche's Songs/Poems," which of course he wants here.

A bit of trouble here with the comparison, the "resemblance" that is being made: "en approachant de" could mean simply "nearing," but then what is the correct meaing of "a s'y/Meprendre"? To be deceived, to be mistaken, or is the intended meaning that in fact what she has said (revealed to him) he interprets as resembling a deception. But whose, his or hers, or both? Is he deceived or mistaken? Difficult to get the correct syntax here when perhaps all the meanings I have stated are intended and there.

Also, "toujours a court d'une bordure" can mean of course just short or shy of a border, edge, frame, meaning, containment, limit or comprehension. I chose "frame" because of the references in other poems to painting, art, sketches and designs, where Roche also talks about the "borders" or frames of works of art.

Then how appropriate is the leap to the Wing of Theosophy, and addressing "Her" directly, the pseudo-science of mystery and spirits and revisiting and reviving ghosts of the past (which he is doing, recalling previous encounters and love sessions and their conversations). This I am certain Roche means to convey here because he uses the outmoded verb "revoler" (Littré). He clearly wants the images of their love to be carried away on the Wings of Theosophy, which in fact then causes these memories and sessions to be conjured up and fly back to him (revoler) as torments, pain, and sorrow. The pain of knowing that while you are loving you must part and everything is already "in the past" and lost to the spirit world of memory and sentiment. And yet they will be "friends," the mundane transformation of lovers by the quotidian.

Pages 76–77: "Les pêcheurs girondins, au moment de franchir le Bec d'Ambez, promettent à la Vierge, qui y a sa chapelle, de ne plus manger de viande le vendredi ni le samedi, mais on assure que lorsqu'ils l'ont passé, ils se hâtent de révoquer leur vœu." From the French website "La Mer" (page 9/9, which presents folktales of France based on the 8 vol. collection by Paul Sêbillot, "Le folklore de France."

This may indeed be the "histoire au Bec-d'Ambez" Roche intends here, where promises made under pain of death or punishment are soon rescinded once the danger has passed.

Some other difficulties here with exact meaning of this poem. How erotic should it be? "Mol élancement" could simply mean tender pain, but I think much more is intended than that. For example, "ton bas-ventre enorme" probably refers in fact to her enormous womb/vagina, but the image of "quittant l'horizon" doesn't quite conform here. At first I had the proper inversion in English: "thy enormous paunch quitting the horizon," but that destroys the line too much, I think, and misses the enjambement/slurred meanings and catachresis. I therefore went with "mons" as holding both sexual idea and "mountain on the horizon," something that could be "stepped from."

"Dêchire-la" could mean "to tear HER apart."

Pages 78–79: *L'Escarpolette* (The Swing) by Jean-Honore Fragonard (1767). I think Roche makes reference to this specific painting because the painting has three (trois) personages in it: the beautiful girl on the swing; the "bishop" who is pushing her from behind (so requested by the lord who commissioned the painting); and the "lord" himself on the ground in front of the swing and girl so that he can have an excellent view of her legs and her et ceterae? There is obviously a ménage a trois implicated here.

Nicolas-Edme Rétif, called Rétif de la Bretonne. October 23, 1734 – February 2, 1806. French novelist.

"Le squelette le la Mort laisse passer les rayons livides de la lumière infernale entre les creux de ses ossements," Chateaubriand, **Mart. 263.**

Pages 90–91: This is a very complex and difficult poem not only to translate but to fully comprehend. The multiple layers of meaning and overlapping conceits are very much in the English Metaphysical vein, except with less coherency and without an overarching conception or "device" that holds the poem and its images together.

Underlying the praise/dispraise of women is the fact that the poet/narrator is again speaking about "having her on her knees" sucking his cock, with which he is "strangling/choking her"; and the double reference to himself and his cock as stiff, ugly stretched out, is evident. He could of course literally be killing her by strangling her to death. The poem then turns direction in the middle to talk of history and accepted Western mores (I think) with the traditional view of woman as idolized, with implied reference to the Virgin Mary ("wood"—a statue of the Virgin?) and also perhaps another allusion to his cock. The two lines beginning with "Qu'il," I have translated the best I could considering the difficulty of pulling coherency out of this poem. "Conceiving in her" is consistent with the sexual content, and perhaps the imperative command "Die!" also refers to the Elizabethan conception of lovemaking as "dying," which occurs in John Donne's poems and also in other poets of the period, including Shakespeare in his sonnets.

Pages 92–93: Definition of "Mentule Marine," from Littré:

"Nom vulgaire d'une sangsue de mer. Lat. mentula, pénis, par assimilation de forme. Aufrecht a donné l'étymologie de mentula; c'est le diminutif du mot qui est dans le sanscrit pramantha, l'agitateur, le bâton qu'on faisait tourner dans le creux d'un morceau de bois pour obtenir le feu; ce bâton est sans cesse comparé dans le Rigvéda à un phallus ; racine manth, agiter."

Trans: "Vulgar name for sea leech. Latin. Mentual, penis, by similarity of shape. Aufrecht gave the etymology of mentula; it is the diminutive of the word pramantha in Sanscrit, the agitator, the stick (baton) that one turns in the slit (or hole) of a piece of wood in order to start a fire; in the Rigveda this baton is continually compared to a phallus; root manth, to agitate (excite)."

I find this is very interesting, considering that Roche refers so frequently to "fire" and "wood." He certainly would know this meaning from the Sanskrit, the stick that one rubs into the slit in another piece of wood to start a fire is compared in the Vedas to a phallus and of course refers to the sexual act. This certainly makes the reference to fires of Bengal more understandable. Of course, Roche also simply means "Ments" to refer to "lies," I assume, or even to "fablements" (fables, myths, lies) with a pun on "faiblement" (weakly).

Pages 116–117: This little poem seems to me to be in imitation of Arnaut Daniel and reminiscent of his poem about his "oncle" and the nail and hare—a play on words and the tour de force of bringing it all off. Here Roche deliberately uses "publication/parution/release of a book or appearance of a thing," "perce," to poke a hole in something, or the verb (pierce), or the noun for the tool which pierces or punches holes (awl or punch in English), with the image to my mind of stitching in book binding. Then he throws in harrow, haven, and the betterave (which could refer, as usual, to his penis). Images of plowing and sowing and growing. Then the image of the Greek fire (burning in water), and also of cooking, a partridge (sans couture?) (seamless), hot (in or out of the pot?), and instructions (enseignement) for who does not kill it (cook it), who does not destroy and partake of the innocent natural thing? A very compact and obscure poem, like two rocks side by side (each stanza). He hoped here, I think, to leave the reader out, but he hasn't, has he?

Page 119: I realize that "méconnaissable" means unrecognizable or unknowable in English, but I like better the alliteration of "misconceived memories." Besides, these really are not unknowable or unrecognizable memories he recounts here, but "ill-formed" or "misshapen" memories.

Pages 122–123: This poem is a derivative of the poem on page 153, which begins with the line "Après déjeuner deux ans après alors qu'il avait." In this poem the lines are deliberately inverted (reversed) with the capitals placed to the right-hand margin of the page. The letters down the right side of the page (right-hand margin) may form an acrostic (anagram), but it would be very difficult if not impossible to duplicate the meaning of the acrostic (anagram) in English and still retain the meaning and sense of the poem. For fun, however, if we first write out the right-margin capitals, we have:

TLLSEAELITEEOGEN

This doesn't seem to me to make any sense at all in either French or English. But Roche also includes some capitals internally on the left margin: Qui, SeS, Si. He also may mean for us to take the entire first word, as follows:

Avait
De
Il
Part
Pareil

Les
Assises
Conduise
Fera (or only A)
De or E
Ondul
Qui
S'ecroulant
Se
Partielle
O
DecouraG
De
J'ar
Posture
Filon
Cale

He may also want to include only the words he has capitalized, which then appear as follows, including those capitalized in the left. To the right I have made a crude speculative translation of these:

Avait	Had
Il	He
Part	Gone
Pareil	As
Les	They
Conduise	Led
FerA	He will make
De	Who
Qui	Ever
Ondul	Undulates
Qui	Who

Ah	Ah
S'ecroulant	Devastating
SeS	Them
Se	Selves
Partielle	Partly
O	O
Si	So
DecouraG(e)	Discouraged
De	With
Posture	Posture
Filon	Rich (rich vein, bonanza)

This, I realize, is all nonsense and made up by me, of course, but a fun word game to play, with endless possibilities. I myself have played this game in a sonnet in my *Mediterranean Sonnets*, before I had ever read or heard of Roche. Such word games of course are nothing unusual:

Sonnet XXII: "Love's Rich Rosary"

Love its rich rosary by rote can read
unsought, not knowing know full Bacchic life
is festival fell brief, whose piping fife
sweet soundings persevere, till winds to reed
ah! couching harmony abjure, or mead
kiss lips past senses' bowl, so frenzy's strife
into her sister's doubling robe as wife
most quick immures, as mothers wheat plump seed.
Thick consequence, heady, profane mischance,
heart-fathers glad germ, live to bulged grain,
O my always new! As smiling foot strike
my eyes to earth unstruck, that ending dance
aways up lift again changed her face like
new looks new buds do take in shaking rain.

I structured this little sonnet so that the first word of each line also makes a little poem, to wit:

Love
unsought
is
sweet
ah!
kiss
into
most
thick
heart
O
my
always
new

And, of course, the first letter of each line forms an anagram of the lover's name.

Pages 124–125: "To many the name of Elsevier represents a prolific modern scientific publishing house. The name perpetuates that of a much older printing dynasty, the house of Elzevier, or Elzevir, which began operating in Leiden in 1580 and continued throughout the Netherlands into the early 18th century.

"While the Elzeviers specialised in accurate editions of classical literature, they were also known for the breadth of their publications. Most of their books were small in size and therefore cheap, the Penguin paperbacks of their time. They were distributed throughout Europe. Soon publications of the house of Elzevier became collectible items."

From the University of London Research Library Services website, regarding their Elezvier Press Collection.

Pages 128–129: One definition from Littré for "toupie" (top, whirligig): Popular: "Femme de mauvaise vie du plus bas étage." This is the first instance in the book where Roche speaks of himself in the persona as narrator/ecrivain, using the first person, "m'en reste," without using the projected voice and image of the "lover/amant" in the poems to this point.

Pages 130–131: Some possibilities for translating "——— nales peurs":

"virginales peurs"=virginal fears (seems very likely)
"diagonales peurs"=crosswise (cross-purpose) fears

Roche may also be thinking in terms (metaphors) of death and decay because of the appropriateness of this idea in context—bubons and impending death and "sinking" (boat tub ferry image) of their love relationship, deformed and cankered by slander and scandal.

The image of the "roe deer" here of course now harkens back to the Song of Solomon, the superlative comparisons of his love to grapes, roe deer (fawns), etc., and the quotation about the beauty and mystery (mysticism) of women's breasts (p. 44).

Re: Rene Crevel and ALCOOLS (d'Apollinaire)
Crevel (1900-1935): Author of *Détours* (1924), *Mon Corps et moi* (1925), *La Mort difficile* (1926), *Babylone* (1927), *L'Esprit contre la raison* (1927), *Êtes-vous fous?* (1929), *Les Pieds dans le plat* (1933), and *Le Roman cassé et derniers écrits* (1934-1935).
Crevel committed suicide in 1935. Found near his corpse was a note on a sheet of paper with a single word: "Dégout" (Disgust). This was rumored to be his last "word" and his suicide note,

but in fact he also left a letter to Tota Cuevas, so "Dégout" was not in fact his "last and only" word.

Page 139: This is Roche's statement about the structure of narration, a direct address to the reader, which should be read in the light of his preface to this collection.

Pages 140–141: This poem has "overtones" of Moby-Dick, with the reference to a "baleine," to sharks, and to the very memorable incident where one of the crew of the *Pequod* puts on and wears as a protective cape the sheath of a whale's penis. In this vein, "Lymne" takes on characteristics, or at least bears some comparison, to Ishmael or a member of the crew of the *Pequod*. The double entendres here are almost disheartening to translate because if you translate literally (the surface meaning) you ignore and miss the sexual undertones. But if you translate the "intended" (sous entendre) sexual meaning, you lose all the fun and sense of the literal. For instance, the difficult lines "Laves qu'elles commettent comme trompettes.../Rincees toujours plus obscures elles vont me suivre," I can translate literally as "Washes that they commit like trumpets/Rinsings always darker they are going to follow me," etc., but the word "lave" in French is the English "lava" and we know he means to call up the gushings and hot flows of puntang that they "emit" (another meaning of "commetter") like trumpets. In this case the noise of trumpets makes more sense. But now if you translate "Rincees" as Rinsings, you lose the sexual power of "dark flows" coming from the volcanoes of women. I also think that "jeter" in this context also has the meaning of ejaculate, where indeed he can be expected to "spurt out very far the amusement (joy) of his first versions." I tried in my translation to take a double route, trying to have it both ways, although admitting, as I do here, that something is bound to be lost.

Pages 144–145: Another difficult poem to translate with all its intended subtle undertones. The idea (to me) of the "tree that falls alone in the forest" and whether or not it makes a sound unheard is inherent here somehow, like a reading or a "version" (lecture) that does not take place (is missing). The difficulty really mounts when the religious aspect of lovemaking is brought in with the line "Tout à coup qui grandit, arbre à demi, fils à" because the rest of the poem plays upon sacrament, Eucharist (cénacle) and religious teaching (moine). I do not know, however, whether "fils" is best translated as "son," "child" or "lines" or "threads." Is "arbre à demi" literally a half grown tree, or does it translate best as I have chosen, "half in bloom"? One may also imply that this poem again refers to his penis, its arc, bending like a tree, etc., which somehow is there but really not explicitly stated, even though the poem ends with "culs," women in alleys behind hotels (prostitutes, I presume), which may also allude to an interlude with a prostitute in a hotel room. The last line may also refer to his penis as like a piece of "cured leather." Remember "passement" earlier in another poem, where leather is "dipped" or cured in a vat. If you don't put in the word "leather," even though it doesn't occur in the French, you run into the problem in English where the word "cured" has two meanings and then makes the translation ambiguous: cured=healthy (which reflects nicely on the use of "Santé," health or well-being) but also cured=prepared by soaking or smoking (like smoked or cured ham). It is probably best, I think, to translate it simply as "like cured," as I have done, but you lose the idea of "cured leather." I also chose to translate "cénacle" as "inner sanctum," even though it means "inner circle" and, when capitalized, "salle de Eucharist." "Inner circle" still might be best because of the idea of the "cunt" and its "inner" circle.

Pages 152–153: This is the "original" poem from which the poem on pages 122-123 derives, which includes a cryptic anagram and arbitrary inversion of lines. This poem, however, makes a very different statement.

Pages 156–157: This poem is like a game of "Jeu d'oie" (continuing from previous poem, pages 154-155), which relies on word play and nonsense that sometimes ends up making very serious and interesting statements, and where chance plays such a prominent role that even near the end the person who is winning can lose. I think I have done a good job of keeping the sense and feeling of the old poem, on the left in italics, a lament for hunger and poverty (and the comparison of the old geezer to a wornout horse no longer able to follow the pack). I also complete the lines of the poem with appropriately corresponding words on the right. To keep the rhyme scheme would be nearly impossible, but I have done the best I can, picking up at least some of Roche's rhymes, bac, sack, track, clac, and fac (faculty). Believe it or not, "usquebac" is actually a word in English (Scottish) for a liquor, and "scubac" is a deliberate alteration of the original word. The word is in Littré, as is usquebac. The word "lie" in French of course means the dregs or bottom stuff of wine (what's in the bottom of the bottle). In English, "lees," which rhymes nicely, but I like "dregs" better for character here. "tombac" in French is metal made of a mixture of copper and zinc. "vie" of course is "life" and I think I have done a nice job of capturing the meaning of meager fare and "ma table est servi." "sac" is bag or sack and I like the way I substituted "port" for "harbor or haven" and retained the continuation of the line, and not too far from the original meaning. To retain the double entendre of his dessert of an "oublie" (a four-cornered folded wafer in French) and the meaning of something "forgotten," I have retained the French word for the wafer.

Pages 172–173: A "tough" little poem. The image of mining ores and minerals is obviously here, as I assume he is "mining" her for her precious ores and minerals. I am not sure what to make out of "La poitrine olive battant le bois ou l'eau" in the context of the various other images and metaphors at work in this poem. And the orgasm like an eyelash after the crocodile? I chose "wink" for "cil" because then at least you have a semblance of meaning. A wink and a nod, eh? I also know that "cent bêtes" could also mean "100 stupidities" but how could these go to the forge with the six merchants? I preferred to put in the "beasts" themselves, which gives the little poem more "mythic" power with "the" six merchants who seem by design linked to them. "Vont à la forge..." may also mean firing up or drawing on the creative energies/fires.

Pages 178–179: I was not certain, at the outset, whether or not to translate "avilissement" as "degradation" or "depreciation," which of course makes a great difference in the meaning of the poem. I do think that this is a poem about degradation and depreciation of their relationship. But later also, the persona talks about "miséricorde" (graciousness) and I suppose the need to follow some sort of "proprieties" in the relationship as it degrades, or is devalued to the status of friendship and "amnesty," a standoff. I also am not certain that "Foulques" should in fact be translated as "coots" or if it is the name of someone, for instance Foulques III Nerra, Le Comte d'Anjou. Is he saying that she (the lover) might hear again the call of the lonely lovebirds if she wanted and/or deserved and needed it again, that is, love and all its moments are still available to her. The image "poissons en enfer" returns rather startlingly to the domestic scene, where she becomes the one who "picks" or "harvests" (recueiller) this devilish fish, with her appalling, frightening, horrible wax fingers, and where does this take place—on the bed. The odor of lovemaking might indeed be governing here at some level, or also to be admitted, the fish from hell could refer even to his phallus, which she no longer comes to "harvest."

Pages 180–181: Another tough little poem, dense, obscure and abstract by concrete detail and reference to particulars that seem to reside "outside" of the poem, but of course this is not possible, as they are resident in the poem. This is a political poem, as so many are in this series about the Library of Congress. The young babies "les chefs de/File" are on the front line of the battlefield (of life?). They are newcomers ("l'arrivant") and their future is to be in "pieces," fragmented and perhaps naively blown up by bombs (?); like front line recruits, they will be materialized, where they are like fodder; but also if they circulate at night looking for forage, they are in grave danger. The poem then shifts to the narrator and his view of his woman/lover and their relation in time and history. The cabin comes in again, the rustic, pastoral setting, as in several places in this collection, with reference to the Greek Baccanales (celebration of Eleusinian mysteries), but for certain the idea here is a fatal idea (néfaste idée) of sacrifice, and my feeling is that it is about of loss of lives in a "providential waste" that must be.

Pages 190–191: Obscure, complex, difficult to know where to go with this one. I don't know if I should translate "Tire du bois" as "call of the woods," "Force of the forest," "pull/draw of the woods/forest" or if the phrase means something entirely different that I am ignorant of. I went with the poetic "Force of the forest" because I like the alliteration, and does the first line really mean "she would return in half an hour"? This problem continues with the meaning of "comment/Cela quel espoir" with the doubling of pronouns. I think he means to "jam" everything together in this poem like a logjam. "ou le biais par lequel y pénétrer" I take in the sexual context (always) to refer to how he "entered her—the slant or way. Should I translate "Dispose l'equipier" literally as "Disposes the mate"? Is also the last line translated correctly? I think that he means to say that they are dreaming of the same thing, not that they are dreaming together of ONE thing. I may be wrong.

The meaning of this tough little poem to me has to do with the realization of the pleasures of sexual intercourse and whether or not these pleasures match our expectations. How do we accurately (precisely) measure this, when the lover is her/himself mixed up with our imposed expectations and the memories already stored in our minds and bodies of previous pleasant and unpleasant encounters. Is this a remembered catalogue of lovers to which he is adding the current relationship and love sessions? What else could he mean by "la série," that is, at least, how I interpret this statement. And in fact he says that the things yet to discover do not in fact exceed their or his fantasy. And the pleasure of dreaming together about the same thing somehow confirms and substantiates this. Always also underlying all of these poems is the idea that the lover is just one in a number and as remarkable and pleasurable as all the current lovemaking is, this is somehow already "in the past." This factor of incipient loss adds to the poignancy of the poems, but also reveals some dishonesty, bitterness, and "hard reality." Pleasures are fleeting and disappearing as they are being enjoyed. Sex itself endures in the moment and in the revitalization through reminiscence, but at the same time, the lover is transitory and no ideal or idol as in past memorializations, like Petrarch's Laura, or the ideal lovers in medieval love poems and romances, or even Dante's religious allegory of love and his apotheosis of Beatrice. Roche knows what he is doing here and he has clear historical heuristics for his "series."

Pages 194–195: The quote from Swinburne is from his *Laus Veneris (Praise of Venus)*, 1866, which has as epigraph a quotation from *Livre des grandes mereilles d'amour, escript en latin et en françoys par Maistre Antoine Gaget*, 1530. In Swinburne's poem to the glory of Venus, after lovemaking with his beloved, the lover laments:

There is a feverish famine in my veins;
Below her bosom, where a crushed grape stains
The white and blue, there my lips caught and clove
An hour since, and what mark of me remains?

Pages 216–217: This poem is "derivative" of the similar poem above (pages 130-131), with wording the same in many places, but with slight differences and changes to make the meaning different. This is not only a play on words and a poet's game, but a way to derive a second (or third) poem of the same experience and condition, and thereby to make the experience a different experience, because the two poems are essentially different, even if only one word or line break is changed.

The use of letters only in the middle of the poem is in fact a type of short hand for the words in the original poem above: i. e., "d p ll s" equals "dépouillées" in the original. "V rm n s" equals "Vermin es" in the original, and "r ng s" (?) = "—nales" in the original above.

Reinier de Graaf—born July 30, 1641, Schoonhoven, Netherlands; died August 17, 1673, Delft. Dutch physician who discovered the follicles of the ovary (known as Graafian follicles), in which the individual egg cells are formed. He was also known for his studies on the pancreas and on the reproductive organs of mammals.

In Littré: DOUCHE, AFFUSION. La douche vient d'une certain distance et a une force d'implusion. L'affusion se fait de près et n'a aucune force d'implusion.

Pages 226–227: Line 6: I like my translation here, which is so nice in English, "Breezes in the night no longer become you," although that may not be the precise meaning in the original.

Line 13: "Emoluement" (*sic*, in original) has the double entendre of "heritage/inheritance?/remuneration?" and moist, slippery, wet. This is difficult to match, but "emollient" is a word in both French and English (the same), and gives the idea, I think, of a slippery/salve/cream. I also realize that "flancs" can be translated as womb (in the singular), but that just doesn't sound right here. And "sides" misses the focus of sexuality. I had at first translated this as:
"…I leave you slip-
Pery like your thighs…" but this finally doesn't seem the best meaning to me.

Pages 230–231: Line 2: I chose "engender" for "se pousse" because I think that the image here is of fecundity (plants and weeds, etc.) growing out of the trash heap of his words (poetry). Engenders seems to convey this better than "grows."

Line 6: I chose "torments" and "sucks" for "harcèle" and "pèle" instead of "peels" or "strips" because stripping or peeling the water away doesn't create the correct image in English. Sucks also occurs later in the poem.

Line 10: "peindre" (to paint) could also be translated as "portrait" but at this point I do not think Roche is talking only about "her" but about the entire poetic he has created about their love and lust. Also, could "la facture/Sur le rebord"mean "the account not settled"? (under construction?), which might make more sense, actually.

Line 15: How to translate "ferrement" to convey both the idea of hardness and "iron" is difficult although I did think of

"Finally if your steely buttocks/Obsess me", which includes both ideas but perhaps is a little too "POETIQUE." I also realize that "immondices" could be translated as "filth" but I like the alliteration of "table of trash".

Pages 248–249: Warloo is a "place" or tribe in Aboriginal Australia, an Aboriginal word that means "fire" or "firewood," and also is referred to as an "evil spirit" (North West of Western Australia). Is it significant (or not) that Roche talks in other poems about "fire," "firestick" and "tire du bois" ("call of the wild" or "shot of wood")?

"The natives' physicians are supposed to be able to cure their illnesses and drive away the evil spirits of other tribes, providing they have not used any exceptional witchcraft. When his attendance is required the physician stands over the patient and groans aloud, and then makes a noise resembling the hushing of a child to sleep. Next, he stands with one foot upon the affected part, and then briskly rubs and squeezes it with his hands. When he considers this massage has been sufficient he puts his mouth over the affected part and proceeds to draw out the evil spirit, calling it a 'Warloo.' After all the evil spirits have been drawn out he runs some little distance with them in his hand and carefully buries them; then be returns, puts his hand to his side, draws out a good spirit, and inserts it into the patient. The physician makes a clicking noise presumably with his fingernails—which the natives of course believe is the spirit being drawn out. When they have rheumatism, neuralgia, or headache they bind the affected part with runners or creepers, but have very few decoctions of herbal remedies."

From *The Customs and Traditions of the Aboriginal Natives of Northwestern Australia,* by John G. Withnell Roebourne, 1901. Scanned as sacred-texts. com, April 2002. Redactor, J. B. Hare.

Pages 254–255: *D'illyrine, ou l'écueil de l'inexperiènce* (1799) by Madame de Morency (1770-1820).

Pages 268–269: "intendants"—district administrators in French, Portuguese, and Spanish provinces. Still a current word. Soissons: "La cité du vase"—Capital of the first Merovingian kings. This city has beautiful architecture from the Middle Ages and the XVIIth and XVIIIth centuries. These include the crypts of the abbeys of Saint-Mêdard and Saint-Lêger, the cathedral of Saint-Gervais-Saint-Protais (a fine example of Gothic architecture in Picardy), and the abbey of Saint-Jean-Des-Vignes, which is the most spectacular monument in Soissons.

Translator's Afterword

Love on the Rocks

I first met Denis Roche in 1978-1979, when I spent a wonderful year in France as Fulbright Lecturer in American literature and culture, and English poetry, at the University of Metz. My assignment was to prepare upper-division French students for the CAPES, the equivalent of a teaching certificate in the United States. Works included on the CAPES examination for this year were Wordworth's *The Prelude*, Theodore Dreiser's *Sister Carrie*, and Saul Bellow's *The Adventures of Augie March*, an odd mix of the Romantic Sublime, Naturalism, and Determinism. If my students came away with no more than an understanding of Augie's inversion of Heraclitus's iron axiom "Character is fate" to "Fate is character," then I think that I may have left them with something to alter their view of reality and existence. What else could I ask? In addition to focusing on these works and authors in my courses, I also taught a special course I organized on 20th Century American Poets and Poetics, for these subjects are nearest and dearest to my heart. It was an excellent choice because I soon discovered that my students knew little about contemporary American poetry and poetics; and this quickly became the most popular course I taught at the university.

All American scholars and students studying in France during this period were, of course, extremely interested in the works of Roland Barthes, Jacques Foucault, Jacques Derrida, Claude Lévi-Straus, Jacques Lacan, and the writers and critics associated with Tel Quel, of whom Denis Roche was a notable member. Besides being a significant poet, author and critic, Roche was also a distinguished editor for Éditions du Seuil and the official French translator of Ezra Pound (*Pisan Cantos* and *ABC of Reading*). It is small wonder, then, that I was immediately taken by his book of poems, *Éros énergumène*, when I found it at my favorite bookstore in Metz on a shelf of works by Tel Quel authors, including the seminal *La Révolution du Poetic* (1974) by Julia Kristeva. I set about immediately to read and translate this significant, ground-breaking collection of poems. Roche's introduction, "Lessons on the Poetic Vacancy," which he calls "fragments," makes patently clear that he has taken poetry in a new direction with the intent of putting an end to both "looked-at" poetry ("Fin de la Poésie Regardée") and "spoken" poetry ("Fin de la Poésie Parlée"). As he explicitly states: "One of the goals of this little book is to show that there can be a poetry that is made neither to be looked at nor to be declaimed. Any poetry that could only be defined by one of these characteristics is but a counterfeit of poetry: 'le lettrisme' has been the counterfeit that one looks at, metric poetry is the counterfeit that one recites aloud."

Roche's new domain, or "realm," for poetry is poetry derived from *pulsion*, an undeniable inner force or energy that drives the poem into being and controls and mandates its origin, source, structure, form, content, rhythm and outcome. This is clearly the reason the erotic takes such precedence and possession of the poetic. It is also quite understandable, with this complex demand for a new poetic where poems are neither viewed nor recited, why Roche would turn to photography and the visual autobiography of his photographs, having perhaps pushed poetry to an absolute limit beyond letter and sound. He has told me personally, however, that this is a meaningless distinction, one only that critics make, because for him there is no difference between the creative acts of photography and writing.

In addition to recognizing that Roche had indeed taken poetry in a new direction, I also understood immediately what he was trying to accomplish, as I had been writing a similar kind of poetry in my *Mediterranean Sonnets*, which I had just completed before coming to France. I knew that we were kindred spirits. I also recognized that Roche was creating a new concept for a book of poems. Robert Duncan and I had often spoken about this subject, as both he and Jack Spicer had deliberately determined to make their books of poems, not loose and unrelated selections of arbitrary individual poems, but a coherent and purposeful collection whose poems all related to each other and presented a unified poetic. This is exactly what I did in *Mediterranean Sonnets*, whose individual poems are all linked to a single vision, structure, and orchestrated impetus. *Éros énergumène* is just such a book of poems. Roche openly abandons both the topical and logical in his book, letting the poems fall where they may as they are written, driven by their inner *pulsion*. This allows the reader to participate actively, intimately, in the creative process and the emotions, pathos and ethos of the poems. Roche obviously invites and accepts fragmentation, experimentation, and the pitfalls, dangers, and marvelous discoveries of digression, chance and error. He plays with calligrams, anagrams, shapes, and word games, willfully breaking up text and subverting tradition and form. He obscures the line between the visual and the written. These are all "motivations" and inventions I also use in *Mediterranean Sonnets* and in my first book of poems, *Corm* (Oyez: Berkeley, 1974).

After struggling through the difficult task of translating the introduction and several of the first poems in the book, with the indispensible help of my good friend Ken McKellar, then teaching English to French students at the University of Metz, I wrote a letter to Denis Roche care of Éditions du Seuil in Paris and included my translations. I asked permission to continue translating the entire book and also to meet him on my next trip to Paris. He kindly replied and told me he liked my translations, and agreed to meet me. On my next trip to Paris, I met him at the offices of Éditions du Seuil, where I was also fortunate to meet Roland Barthes as he was coming down the stairs. Roche and I had a lively and entertaining lunch and immediately became friends. He gave me permission to translate the entire book of poems, and when he asked why I wanted to complete that arduous task, I replied that I felt obligated to present his book as "book" and remain faithful to its structure and *pulsion*. We both smiled at this mutual understanding. I communicated with him several times throughout my term as Fulbright Lecturer, and we saw each other again as I was leaving France to return to California. He signed my copy of *Éros énergumène* with the following inscription:

> *Pour Frank, qui part en*
> *Californie, moi je serai*
> *bientôt à Naples. Et il m'a*
> *promis un tour dans sa*
> *Chevie 1941 quand j'irai*
> *le vois.*
>   *A bientôt*
>   *Denis*

Little did I know at the time that it would take me so long to complete my translation of this wonderful and important book of poetry. After completing the entire translation, I sent the manuscript to Roche and Éditions du Seuil, who kindly gave me the rights for the English publication.

Roche and I met again in Paris in June 2009 when we renewed our friendship. Although he was then retired from Éditions du Seuil, he was still very active as photographer and writer. We spoke again of many subjects near and dear to our hearts: our friendships with contemporary poets, the state of poetry in the 21st century, Seamus Heaney, Ezra Pound and Robert Duncan. As I walked him to his taxi, and we hugged each other before he got in and parted—waving to me with his cane through the side rear window—he reminded me that I still owed him that promised ride in my 1941 Chevy.

Unfortunately, Denis Roche died on September 2, 2015, before he could see the publication of my translation of *Éros énergumène*, and sadly before I could give him the promised ride in my 1941 Chevy.

Frank Cebulski
Albany, California
February 14, 2017, Valentine's Day